SHATTERING THE BELIEF CODE

How to Change the Beliefs Which Prevent You from Discovering, Transforming and Igniting Your True Self

WENDI FRANCIS MS, RD, CPC

"Wendi uses an amazing process to help her clients utilize their abilities to cultivate permanent change. Her insight to get right to the heart of the matter is like no other person I have worked with before.

Her listening skills, proven strategies and gentle, yet firm guidance has immensely helped me see what I needed to do to get my life on track. I have learned what I need to do to incorporate lasting change, and how to hold myself accountable for my present and future. Wendi is an incredible coach! I am so happy I got to work with her. It changed my life!"

-Elena S.

"I have had the pleasure to be a client of Wend Francis for four years. Throughout this time, she has had amazing insight helping me re-frame situations and helping me place them in proper perspective.....there has never been a visit with her that I did not leave with clarity and thorough notes!

Last year my mother was diagnosed with terminal cancer. I credit a lot of my strength and determination to Wendi. Her vast knowledge and expertise in grief has carried me through. I am so fortunate to have her in my circle. She is an extraordinary human being who shows much compassion and understanding for her clients."

-Stephanie S.

"She spoke from her heart and she saved my life...literally."

-Dru M.

"I find my coaching session with Wendi to be like talking to my best friend. That person that you can instantly be completely vulnerable with and be 100% yourself, with no fear of being judged...but rather accepted exactly as you are. Wendi leads me toward developing action plans to achieve my most important goals. She is a talented coach who also leverages her background to help you understand how some past experiences could be presenting obstacles to success. Her comprehensive approach is not only effective, but she is kind, loving and genuinely cares about her clients. I'll be forever grateful that God led me to coach with Wendi!"

-Lisa K.

"Simply put, Wendi is outstanding! Her perceptiveness and professionalism saw me overcome a family crisis with clarity and purpose, heal my heavy heart, and embrace the journey of being grateful. Now I'm equipped with strategies and once again am inspired about life, my passions and am rising to a whole other level."

-Sue C.

"Wendi has always had a wealth of knowledge in the expertise of working with clients to help them see a different view of their food issues. The ability that she has shown to aid in the healing process for so many people by reframing their perspective of issues they have dealt with most of their lives has been a gift to so many individuals that she has worked with.

It is remarkable how many nutritionists simply approach clients from a perspective of food planning, and how instead she approaches their food issues from a developmental perspective that helps people see where they developed their beliefs in the first place, and how to shift their view to an adult view instead of the view they grew up with. I want to thank her for working with so many clients and helping their healing process. The clients she has worked with have been so lucky to be blessed with her gifts as a professional."

-Ann Kreindler-Siegel, LCSW, MSW, MAEd, SEP

"There is no doubt in my mind I would be living the healthy and HAPPY life I am today without Wendi as my guide. Her calming presence and direct approach made it possible for me to open up and deal with what was uncomfortable. I was able to listen and trust that Wendi truly wanted the best for me. She never overwhelmed me with ways I needed to change or focus on what needed to change. Instead Wendi challenged me in a way that was caring and empowering, and in return made recovery possible."

-Carrie M.

'Wendi Francis has the rare ability to tune into what is happening in one's life and meet that person "where they are" on their journey. She can help him/her process issues that need reframing, and walk the person step by step through potential options for healing and growth. Wendi's compassionate, loving nature is evident and palpable in all she does. She has assisted me numerous times in my own path to self-acceptance, and encouraged me to take risks and follow my dreams'.

-Hope Gold, MA, CHLC, University Instructor

'Wendi's passion and enthusiasm for helping her clients is enormous. Her ability to help any client truly transform the beliefs they hold is amazing. She is a highly skilled practitioner enabling her clients to make true lasting change in both their personal and professional lives.'

-David Brownlee, CPC, Coach, Author, Speaker

"Wendi has many gifts. One of her main gifts is to be able to connect and be effective with her clients including the ones more stuck in their unhealthy patterns. How she does that, is by being forthright, open and honest. She helps her clients examine their thoughts and become aware of their faulty thinking. She teaches them to find balance and clarity. She understands resistances and works in a way that so respectful, that they are willing to let go of their stories."

—Laura Bass MSW, LCSW

If you need an expert guide, mentor, teacher, or friend to help you problem-solve in life or are needing direction in relationships, life transitions, business, finding purpose, parenting, health issues, or spirituality (amongst many more), get in touch with Wendi Francis. Be prepared find clarity to see life and yourself differently in a short amount of time. She will help you build confidence to make changes in your life that you did not think possible. With Wendi as your guide, you will find your wings to soar and create a happier, richer life than you could have ever imagined!"

-Betsy Wallace Browder

AUTHOR'S NOTE

In this book, I use examples of clients I have worked with from my own private practice or in workshops I have conducted. In order to protect their privacy and ensure confidentiality, I have changed their names, descriptions and other identifying factors. I am extremely grateful to them for their examples and their trust in me and truly honor them for their courage in shattering their belief code.

I have not changed the names of any members of my family or of any examples that include myself or my family.

Copyright © 2015 Wendi Francis

All Rights Reserved

All content is subject to copyright and may not be reproduced in any form without express written consent of the author.

Although the author and publisher have made every effort to ensure that the information in this book was correct at press time, the author and publisher do not assume and hereby disclaim any liability to any party for any loss, damage, or disruption caused by errors or omissions, whether such errors or omissions result from negligence, accident, or any other cause.

This book is not intended as a substitute for the advice of medical professionals. The reader should regularly consult a medical professional in matters relating to his/her health and particularly with respect to any symptoms that may require diagnosis or medical attention.

Cover Illustration, Book Design and Production by Efluential Publishing, a division of eFluential Marketing, LLC.

ISBN-13: 978-1511938365 Paperback

www.EfluentialPublishing.com

DEDICATION

This book is dedicated to my amazing clients that have honored me by choosing me as their practitioner and allowing me to learn from, grow with and transform over the past 20 years. Your courage and dedication to change within yourself has always been an inspiration to me and has continued to push me to grow and learn so that I can serve and help you at the highest level.

In special dedication to my dear friend, Robyn Ebelherr, who has displayed tremendous courage and massive change in her belief systems in order to serve her child, family and the world by changing the way the world views children with Down's Syndrome. Keep it up girl, the world WILL take notice.

To understand more of Robyn's journey with her daughter Sage view http://dsacharlottesville.wordpress.com or contact me directly at www.empowermentcoachinginternational.com

PREFACE

In writing this book as a working mom of three, I came upon four weeks of time where each family member in my house got sick. The flu, congestion, coughs and colds flooded our house leaving me sleepless and too tired to work on this book. Every time I went to begin writing someone else would get sick, either one my children, myself or my husband. I, once again was challenged to hold onto the teachings in this book as I multi-tasked through many different parts of my life, as many of us do. During this time I needed to help my children with their health and emotional needs, my clients with their physiological and psychological needs and work by myself in writing this book, re-launching my website, working through specific issues with family and friends and taking care of myself physically and emotionally as well.

I did not write this book "in a bubble", I wrote this book in and with my life. As I sit here reworking and editing this book on 2 hours of sleep, after my son was up all night with the flu, I realize again how important the contents of this book are. I also, once again, think about how much I can relate to and understand any individual who has multiple facets of focus in their lives that need attention.

I write this only to let you know as a mother, a woman and a professional I truly know, understand and empathize with others who have various parts to their life and who still find the courage, strength and stamina to persevere and take their lives and those around them to another level. I have had and will continue to have times of struggle. The difference is that now I know what I know these times will ultimately lead to times of prevailing.

This book is written for anyone else who wants to continue learning on their journey and has a belief that is holding them back in their life that they want to transform to find their mission, vision and purpose and ignite their true self.

CONTENTS

Introduction 3

Chapter 1: The Quintessential Understanding of Empowerment 7

Chapter 2: Empowered Parenting: A Different Option...... 21

Chapter 3: The Ultimate Lack of Empowerment: Generational Disempowerment and Trauma ... 27

Chapter 4: Deconstructing the Belief Code: Identifying and Understanding Your Beliefs and How They Affect Your Ability to Connect to Your True Self 37

Chapter 5: The Link Between Beliefs and Emotions 57

Chapter 6: Fear and Shame Based Beliefs: A Slippery Slope 63

Chapter 7: The Meanings of Our Lives 73

Chapter 8: Putting It All Together: The EBM System (Emotions, Beliefs and Meanings) 77

Chapter 9: Turning Disempowerment Around: The
"How To" Guide to Empowerment 83
Grounding 85
Orienting 88
The OR Process 89
Discovering and Uncovering Beliefs 95
The EBM Process 99

Chapter 10: Your Next Steps and Resources 103

About the Author 105

WITH GRATITUDE

"Gratitude is the memory of the heart."
– Jean Baptiste Massieu

First and foremost, I want to thank my husband, Charlie, and children, Kaiya, Akoda and Banyan, for supporting me on this journey in writing my first book as well as supporting, loving and encouraging me through all that I and we have done in the past years. You all are the core of my love and the center of my soul.

To all of my friends and colleagues who have supported me during this writing process and throughout my personal and professional journey and lessons in my life.

Last but by no means least, to my biological family—my mother and father for bringing me into this world and for teaching me so many valuable lessons, my grandfather for being my rock and my eternal optimist, my Aunt Ann for your bright smile, my cousin Gary for our shared DNA, my cousin Robbie for your perpetual energy, and my "Texas" family.

Thank you, thank you, thank you. Without all of you I truly would not be the person I am today.

INTRODUCTION

GETTING TO KNOW ME AND WHY I WROTE THIS BOOK

"The Story of My Life"
- One Direction

My intention in writing this book is twofold. First is to allow you individually to know that no matter what you believe about yourself, your life and your world, you can identify and transform it and your life. This will ultimately allow you to ignite a spark that will carry you on to find your true self. Second is to teach what I have learned, enabling other professionals to add immense value to their clients and their practice.

Growing up I was raised by my mom, alone, as she divorced my father when I was very young. Both my mother and father abused alcohol. My mother has also struggled with mental illness, chronic pain and prescription pain medication addiction. Although the apartment complex and the environment I grew up in provided me a community, it also taught me many lessons around emotional abuse, physical abuse, murder, death, rape, rage and alcohol/drug addiction. In looking back, I know the way I have become the person I am today is centered around the beliefs I held during that time.

In growing up and leaving this community, I developed more beliefs that would allow me to soar through undergraduate and graduate school, marry an amazing man and start my private practice and my family. In 2010, three years of an emotionally trying time began constituted by our office manager and friend passing from cancer, our daughter having a tumor removed, our research, discovery and implementation of treatment for this tumor, my delving into the realm of homeschooling, my grandfather passing away from kidney cancer and a host of other smaller things I and we endured during this time.

In 2013, I realized that I had become disempowered in some negative beliefs that I had unconsciously constructed during this time. I was apathetic, reactionary and irritable. I had cared for so many others during this time I had forgotten how to take care of me. It was time to break free from these and own myself again, outside of being a mother and a wife.

Ironically, during this time, my stepmother, who was passing away from cancer, confronted me lovingly and said, "You are amazing at what you do professionally. Why are you hiding behind your role of being a mother? I know being a mom is very important to you but it is also important that you get your gifts and talents into the world. Stop hiding and get out there, kid!" She was absolutely right; it was time to find "all of me" again.

Professionally speaking I have been on an amazing journey since deciding to specialize in eating disorders at age 20. Since then I have been learning and growing personally and professionally to help clients who are living in disempowerment. Clinically speaking, I am a registered and licensed dietitian with a graduate degree and specialized training in eating disorders, feeding issues, trauma, somatic experiencing, grief/loss, internal family systems, nutrition, detoxification, and alternative health/ healing pathways. I am also certified as a Professional Life Coach and a Neuro-Linguistics Practitioner. At this point in my career I work with all types of clients, combining all areas of my expertise to enable clients to truly transform their disempowered lives both personally and professionally. In working and teaching many professionals over the last 10 years I realize how many do not know about or understand how to work with beliefs and facets of empowerment. As a professional, I want to be able to train other professionals how to use this work to immensely impact their clients' lives.

It is easy to keep disempowering beliefs, especially because many people do not even know what their beliefs are. Yet, it is these beliefs that provide the foundation for our lives. They stem from our stories and create meanings and emotional links. Whether you are a mother, father, son, daughter, business man or woman, professional, non-professional, hero, survivor or heartthrob, you have beliefs. In those beliefs you hold the key to your unconscious and conscious mind. Unlocking this key unlocks your world and truly transforms how you think, feel and act.

This past year and a half I have worked extremely hard on my own beliefs and empowerment. In that, I have found a renewed strength and talent and have helped others more personally and professionally than I could have ever done before. I am on a solid foundation of empowering beliefs, and by reading this book you can discover what your beliefs are and truly transform them and yourself into a more amazing you.

My intention in writing this book is to help you understand what empowerment is, how disempowerment occurs and how to turn your and your clients' disempowerment around by using their belief construct in their brain and body to do so. This truly allows you and your clients to live in choice and action versus reaction and to be aligned and congruent in your body, mind and soul. It is my part in fulfilling my belief that I was born unto this earth to be there for others and help them in all and any ways that I can by allowing you to learn through my experience and lessons, both professionally and personally. It's written for professionals and lay people alike, parents, survivors, heroes, mothers, daughters, business men, business women, housewives and house husbands. It is written for anyone who wants to learn how to change the beliefs which prevent you from discovering, transforming and igniting your true self, professionally or personally. It is written for you. Here is to learning, growing and living an empowered life— enjoy!!

CHAPTER 1

THE QUINTESSENTIAL UNDERSTANDING OF EMPOWERMENT

> "I hear and I forget, I see and I remember, I do and I understand."
> – Confucius

Over the last 20 years of practice I have brought up empowerment hundreds of times. Inevitably the majority of the time my client will say, "What is that?" In the simple sense of the word, empowerment is the acceptance of one's own personal power or authority. In a culture that has so many choices, it is interesting to me that we do not know more about and exactly what empowerment is.

The core foundation of the definition of empowerment is *the process of increasing an individual's ability to make choices and to transform these choices into desired actions or outcome.* Empowerment allows a person to sit in action versus reaction, to act in choice rather than react out of emotion. It defines a person's present reality because it allows them the ability to feel they are "steering their own ship"; knowing that you are truly in charge of your own life without being at cause, feeling like "things are happening to you." In empowerment you know that all things are happening for you as you are designing or creating them in the choices that you make.

Disempowerment can be something we create ourselves, others create for us or it can be generational. Truly looking objectively at your own places of disempowerment and recognizing where, when and how your choices became narrowed is truly imperative in allowing you to understand the origin of your disempowerment. This allows you to look at the present day and create all of your choices, linking them to your true outcome or results, something that I call OR.

True empowerment does not rely on the mind alone, and what it thinks or feels, but it also relies on the body. Dr. Peter Levine, who has studied trauma extensively for over 40 years, states that true empowerment embodied comes from a person's body being "resourced, grounded and centered, resilient, able to experience healthy aggression and being able to move away from danger." Since we are not just a mind or a body it makes complete sense that what affects the body affects the mind as well. So, trauma in effect produces perceptual changes as well as changes in how we feel in our body. Working through this trauma allows someone to move into empowerment.

In being empowered and truly making your own choices you are also able to shield yourself from trauma in both the present and future. Living a life by empowered design allows you to know in the moment where you are going, thus renegotiating any trauma that may have occurred in your past. Living in choice truly allows you to shield future trauma, as this puts you at cause versus effect. Empowerment allows you to flow in your intention and not be emotionally charged in your choices. Attaching to the emotion related to the result allows you to be in choice. Being emotionally charged in your choices puts you in reaction which does not allow you to be in choice.

When we make choices emotionally charged, we will have results that are emotionally charged. Buying a car or a pair of jeans because of the way it makes us feel can lead to financial issues. On a more serious note, making choices in an emotional charge is truly one of the ways that trauma, grief and loss can occur. Going out for a drive when one is radically upset can lead to devastating consequences.

Empowerment also allows individuals to focus on their desired actions or outcomes. This is truly different than making goals. Goal writing is an act. Outcome or Result writing, a process I call OR, focuses on creating your desired actions or outcomes while in choice, which is an empowered, proactive ACTION. Defining a desired action or outcome is choice based and emotionally driven from a present moment perspective. It is not based on a past or future moment perspective. This allows the individual to be truly attached to the end result and have the internal motivation to succeed. It also encompasses an individual's capacity to store this information in their body, by doing this process from a grounded and centered space and to anchor it within their body as well. This brings in all capacities of a person's ability to store and change. Please see the OR writing section in the last chapter of this book for more details.

> *Kirsten, a psychologist and small business owner, came to our coaching sessions with a goal of growing her business by 50,000 dollars in the next year and expanding her practice to two other sites in the southeast. In looking at Kirsten's entire wheel of life and world I knew that at this point in her life she was in complete choice orientation. She was resourced,*

oriented and grounded and was truly ready to make change. In our first session we, together, determined and designed her outcome/result for this process in specific detail. (Please read OR to see how this process is done at the end of the book.)

Once she knew specifically what her outcome/result was and had a complete list of her choices our work began to move forward. Four sessions later, Kirsten had hired an amazing CFO, developed, expanded and implemented her marketing calendar and begun the process for research and development for her third of the four business sites.

Personally, during this time, we also segmented her schedule and allowed her to get regularly scheduled personal time within her work schedule, which allowed her to work on herself while she was working on the business. This, in fact, is one of small business owners' downfalls. If the owner/ visionary does not take specified time to work on themselves and work "on" the business, they will forever be working "in" the business. Working ON your business instead of IN your business will bring you the true title of entrepreneur versus owner.

Interesting to notice as well is that as a client becomes more empowered, so does their world and universe around them. In Isaac Newton's words, "For every action, there is an equal and opposite reaction." Circumstances present themselves in alignment with my clients' outcomes/results, people show up to help out and various other opportunities transpire. For Kirsten, these things began to show up in the form of marketing events transpiring, employees stepping up to take over roles in the practice, and a CFO literally presenting himself out of nowhere. True individual empowerment leads to universal empowerment. Where "focus goes energy flows" and in focusing your energy on your empowerment, you will see your world, business or personal or both, open up to ALL the possibilities.

> Kyra, a woman with restrictive anorexia, came to me upon the referral of her doctor and therapist. She had been sober for three years but currently was declining steadily in her weight and had radical dehydration from lack of significant fluid intake.
>
> During our initial session I began to get some insight into her story and her sense of empowerment and beliefs. As we worked together her hydration and her ability to consume fluids increased. (She restricted both food and fluids alike, something I know to happen for a subset of the population with Restrictive Anorexia.) She began to work wholeheartedly on her food restriction. After two years of treatment she conquered her fear of nourishing her body, feeding herself regularly and achieving empowerment in her food.
>
> During the final stages of this process, however, issues with her husband arose and they began intense marital counseling. In keeping her grounded and focused on empowerment in health maintenance she was able to maintain her eating during this process and not relapse into her anorexia. She used the issues with her husband as a fuel for her empowerment versus a reason to decline.
>
> As her husband decided he no longer wanted to be married, they separated. Although she spiraled some emotionally, we worked hard together to focus on what she wanted in choice, emotional state management and

future vision. She got a job at a large company and is now getting ready to move to an area where she will feel more supported. She has been and continues to nourish and feed her body regularly and consistently and has not fallen back into her patterns of depression or anorexia. Not to mention during this time she also stopped smoking to increase her health status.

During our last session, as we spoke about the changes she was making, she stated her belief she had been using to get her through to that point. "I am trying." I knew that this belief had helped her radically up until this point but to go to the next level she would need to adapt a new belief. In that moment I said to her, "You know what, Kyra, you are not trying, YOU ARE DOING!" After a momentary pause, she said to me, "You know what, Wendi, you are right, I am doing!"

That is true empowerment, knowing that you are in action, not reaction. Owning your own choices and making decisions that are focused on your ultimate outcome/result. Continually focusing on the present and future actions that allow you to stand in choice and that will lead to your ultimate vision. Kyra has a vision of success for herself and her life and continues to blossom, allowing her to stay empowered.

Notice that as I described Kyra at the beginning of the case study, I did not call her an "anorexic." I mentioned her as a client WITH anorexia. I believe that diagnosis and labeling, as such, is truly a way that we disempower our clients. Diagnosis is a true label of disempowerment. It encourages clients and other practitioners to look at the clients as their symptoms and not as the person they are inside, wholly and completely. It presents them with a disempowered identity that labels them, not encouraging choice or option for client and definitely not encouraging future vision without this identity or label. Focusing on differentiating between diagnosis and person is essential in empowerment and allows the client to find and see themselves for "who they are" not "what they do."

A One-Way Road to Empowerment: Emotional State Pattern Empowerment

Ultimately, for all individuals, having choice in your state of mind is true empowerment. *A person's emotional state pattern is comprised of their internal language or self-talk, physiology, focus and emotion.* Looking at these four facets of any individual allows you to truly understand their psychology in the moment. For individuals who are truly resourced, oriented and grounded this can provide a tool for them to manage their state and stay in choice around their emotions, not allowing them to be swept away emotionally.

Internal Language/Self-Talk: This is how we talk to ourselves in the moment. It is our internal dialogue. For example: "I am so good at this" or "I am always messing things up."

Physiology: This is two-faceted. One facet of physiology is external physiology. This is how an individual stands or sits, breathes, walks, talks, holds their head and neck and holds their facial muscles in a certain emotional state. In general it would be how an individual looks physically when they are in a certain state. Are they hunched over? Are they breathing fast or slow? Do they have their fists clenched?

The other facet of physiology is how an individual feels inside their body when they are in a certain emotional state. Do they feel butterflies in their chest? Do they feel energy in their arms? Do they feel weak or wobbly legs? These physical patterns of energy determine where, when and how this emotional state is stored and anchored in a person's body. It can be linked back to certain emotional states and can be released accordingly as well.

Focus: This is what we focus on in an emotional state. It may be what we focus on in the moment or it may also be what we focused on in the past or in our stored memories we have and can be either a physical or emotional focus. Do you focus on the anger in someone else's face? Do you focus on the beauty of the sunset? Do you focus only on your own anger? Focusing on aspects of the past are defined as a "resourced" focus.

A resourced focus is a stored memory that an individual has that is linked to an emotional state. For example, in my stored memory I have exact moments of hitting a field hockey ball with my stick. It is in these moments I felt strong, powerful and youthful. I regularly access these memories if I need to access these emotions. This could also be a view from a window where someone was vacationing or a scowl on their mother's face right after they were hit with a belt. You do not need to actually create these emotions; you already have a link to them in the stored crevices of your mind.

Emotion: This is a true emotion the individual feels in this state that they identify. It may be in their own language; rage, frustration, fear, anxiety. I have found many times in my career in working with these patterns that the emotion I would have linked with the other top three legs of the clients table does not always match the emotional leg I would have guessed. That is why it is so important to gain clarity around this.

Here is the easiest way to think of an emotional state. I love to educate my clients about this as well to further aid them in their understanding of empowerment. Think of your emotional states like a table with four legs.

EMOTIONAL STATE

| EMOTION | FOCUS | LANGUAGE | PHYSIOLOGY |

Each one of these legs holds up the table of emotional state. Each of these legs can be identified, described, understood and ultimately changed or renegotiated to empower a client to know that they are truly in choice around their emotional state. In fact, in focusing your energy on these four things, you truly put your energy toward aspects you CAN change instead of putting your energy into things you cannot change. In my work with clients, I have most often found that each client has a specific "inroad" to their emotional state. This means that they can identify and transform one area easier than the others. This varies from client to client and can be identified in experimenting and processing with each client individually.

A male client of mine, Mark, was working with his wife in marriage coaching with me. In the third session he identified an emotional state that came up frequently for him when he was running late for work. Working together, we drew his table. Here is what it looked like.

FRUSTRATION

STRESS, ANGER	ON FLOOR IN FRONT OF HIM OR ON CLOCK	"I HAVE TO GET TO WORK" "I WILL BE BEHIND ALL DAY"	HUFFING/PUFFING CLENCHED FIST HUNCHED OVER TIGHTENED STOMACH

Through coaching, he came to the realization that the easiest leg for him to work with was his physiology. I actually call this the clients "inroad." This is the place that they can go into their pattern and change it. His breathing patterns were intense, huffing and puffing, his shoulders became hunched over, he felt tension in his stomach and he would begin pacing around the house.

In working together we designed a physiological pattern interrupt that he could adopt when he got into this pattern. A pattern interrupt is something that stops the cycle of an emotional, cognitive or physical pattern by interrupting its process. This is very similar to a stop sign in the middle of the road for a car. First, he focused on slowing his breath down and then changing his posture. Next, he began walking slower and slower to reduce his pacing around the house. The first time he did this, he realized how much just slowing down his walking helped him focus more on the present moment and quelled his frustration with being late for work. Over time, while practicing, he began more and more to realize how much he could choose his emotional state by playing with and changing his physiological pattern. We did later work with the other legs of his table and redrew those as you can see below. However, for Mark, his physiology was always his primary portal into his state that he continues to use to empower himself to this day.

ACTIVE HELPER HUSBAND

| CALM | ON WHAT'S AROUND HIM / MY CHILDREN, MY WIFE | "IT WILL BE OK" / "IT WILL WORK OUT" | BREATHE DEEPLY / SHARE OUT FIST/LOOSEN / STAND UP RIGHT |

In core connections, particularly marriages or parent/child relationships, our emotional state patterns also affect others' emotional state patterns.

In working with Mark and his wife, Evelyn, she identified her own emotional state and pattern that Mark's would trigger for her as well. We began to work with her emotional state that happened in response to Mark's, which allowed them to understand each other's states and patterns. I educated each of them with the others assistance on their patterns and working with various pattern interrupts that would empower themselves and their partner. This allowed both Mark and Evelyn to understand each other's states and patterns and to recognize what they did to trigger each other's as well. We further worked on where and when these patterns began, their emotional links and the beliefs behind these patterns.

In our next call, Evelyn identified something that was even more interesting. "I realized when we were visiting Mark's mom and dad, that his dad had the exact same physiological patterns when he was frustrated with work." This was an excellent learning tool for both Mark and Evelyn and a fantastic example of generational emotional state patterns as well.

Identifying and understanding the four components of emotional state truly empowers individuals in their lives. Identification is not meant to take away the emotional state. However, it does allow an individual to know they can recognize this state and change it. More than that, it truly allows for choice in emotional state versus reaction to your environment. This tool allows people to harness their emotions so that they can maintain their state when needed and it allows for a deeper understanding of the specific emotion as well. As I say to all of my clients, your emotional state and its four components are truly the things you CAN control in your world. Putting your energy toward understanding and working with the components of your emotion truly works FOR you instead of AGAINST you in taking your energy away and giving it to others in trying to control their actions. The only other two things that one can truly control are your own philosophy and your own actions.

The areas that we can control and put our energy toward in all situations are your

1. Internal Language
2. Physiology
3. Emotion
4. Focus
5. Philosophy
6. Actions.

In focusing your energy on any or all of these six aspects you truly empower yourself by harnessing and using your energy in ways that can positively impact your situation.

Emotional State Empowerment can also open up new and better connections between spouses, families and children alike, as well as deepening our understanding and our connections we have within ourselves.

Furthermore, each emotional state we have leads to each "identity" we hold. Identifying the emotional states that are related to different identities allows you to fully know each of your identities, their emotional state facets and when/where you use them. This allows you to identify and change between each identity you have smoothly and quickly. For example, when I am working with clients I hold a very different emotional state pattern than when I am playing with my three-year-old. In knowing both of these emotional state patterns I can transition from one to the next just like putting on and taking off different hats.

CHAPTER 2

EMPOWERED PARENTING: A DIFFERENT OPTION

> "Together we will cry and face fear and grief. I will want to take away your pain, but instead I will sit with you and teach you how to feel it."
> – *Daring Greatly* by Brené Brown

For the last twenty years in practice, I have heard parents of my clients with eating disorders say to me, "fix her," "make her eat." In an eating disorder much of the treatment is focused not on empowering clients by choice but in taking away choices. My focus on treating these individuals is giving them loving, nurturing choices within boundaries in their food and teaching them how to express their emotion without using food as their language. Eating disorder treatment is complex and multifaceted and probably the topic for another book. However, my concern always for my clients is within their disempowered family infrastructure or within their own infrastructure if they live alone.

In order to "help" their children, parents and sometimes practitioners of my clients begin taking away choices, focusing only on the result or outcome of weight gain. The family pinpoints the person with the eating disorder as the one "with the problem" in the family. Yet, we know within the family dynamic that the person with the eating disorder is the person who is acting out the symptom of the disease within the family.

The outcome or result of weight gain is truly disempowering for a person with an eating disorder because it is the one thing they are desperately afraid of. Making a person with an eating disorder eat or gain weight truly is like saying to someone, "Let's put you in front of a moving train and see how it feels." It is a war within their brain. Yes, for a client with anorexia they really ARE that afraid of gaining weight. The inevitable fear-based reaction present for the client in fight/flight reactions, anxiety or depression.

What I have learned from this is that to help any child with a chronic illness it is most important to allow them to be empowered in their world. Chronic illness can be anything from eating disorders to cancer to diabetes. Empowered parenting techniques allow the child or adolescent to feel like they have a choice in their world and also allow them to own and know they have an impact on their outcome. This radically reduces their fear and decreases their anxiety knowing they have a sense of empowerment (choice = outcome/result).

Guidelines for Empowered Parenting
1. As the parent, research and develop a list of ALL of the options for success. For older adolescents include them in the research when appropriate. Whether this be for a child's treatment or for their success in school, it allows both you as the parent and eventually, essentially, the child, to have all available choices.
2. Speak to the child about all the choices within the limits or boundaries that you have available to you or are that

are within reasonable limitations for their age. Allow them to be involved in as many of the choices as possible with open dialogue at an age-appropriate level. Realize and recognize that how and what you speak to a six-year-old is different from how and what you would speak to a sixteen-year-old about. Remember to keep *all* choices that you have researched, though, to enable you as the parent to continue to feel empowered and know that there are other choices if needed in the future.

3. Create an expanded outcome or result together with the child looking at everything physically, mentally, emotionally and spiritually that will result from this action. When we did this for my daughter, Kaiya, in her treatment for a tumor, this meant short-term and long-term health goals, greater energy for gymnastics which she loved, different experiences and travel, expanding her learning of her body physically and increasing our learning as a family as well. Now as a parent my outcome or result was to eradicate any possibility that this tumor would return. But for Kaiya we linked it into the things listed above and got even more specific as we knew when, where and how treatments were going to be completed.

4. Bring the issue/illness into the family infrastructure. This could be changing the family's eating patterns together, changing family exercise patterns together or taking supplements together. For my daughter this was doing the majority of her nutritional, detoxification and rebuilding protocols with me, my husband and my son as well.

5. Keep out of blame, shame or guilt. Know that this is not your fault but it is your obligation to help heal. Work with and eradicate your own disempowered beliefs as a

parent and stay in empowerment during the process. Be real and vulnerable with your emotions to yourself and others. Whether it is bad grades or a chronic illness we, as parents, always tend to have emotions attached to the outcome. Stay in empowerment around these emotions and know that the more you stay empowered the more your child will feel and be empowered as well. Staying stuck in shame, guilt, fear, blame, anger or worry will not allow you or your child to overcome the issue at hand. Know when, where or if you need an extended support system such as a therapist, coach or other mental health care provider.

6. Finally, and most importantly, make it FUN. Whenever possible, make a game out of the learning or make the learning a fun process. Remember this is the game of life and learning lessons is the biggest part of it. Allowing children to have fun in the learning process allows them to associate positive feelings with change versus negative feelings, enabling both them and you to want to continue to change, learn and grow forever. As a family, we made a game out of learning to take vitamin pills, we played who can fill the urine jug up more and we laughed at the silly faces we made as we took some of our supplements.

Through my clients I learned and developed these principles and through my daughter's illness I lived them. When Kaiya's tumor was removed and we began to develop treatment, detoxification and supplementation protocols I included her on everything that was age appropriate. I allowed her to know what we were doing and why, I sat with her through her fears and I embraced all the protocols from a family perspective. I will forever be grateful to my most amazing son, Akoda, who did the vitamin supplementation protocols with his sister. We learned as a family, in a game I created, how to take vitamin pills together. We made it part of our family routine to complete whatever protocol we were doing. We got our blood tested together for nutritional deficiencies, drank and ate new and different foods together and laughed together as we created a game out of peeing in a jug for 24 hours to get urine testing done for all of us.

When we finally went to Spain for treatment I did all of the treatments with my daughter that I could and sat with her when I couldn't do them myself. My husband researched adventures we could take as a family together so the main outcome of our trip to Spain was not just to receive treatment for Kaiya's tumor but to have an amazing family experience, allowing Kaiya to be relieved of any facet of negative emotion linked to this experience. When we got our blood tested in Spain we all did it and looked at the results together with the doctor. We made the process of her healing "our" learning instead of "her" problem, ultimately empowering her to feel loved and supported, knowing that we would be there for her in her fear or worry and that we could truly understand what she was going through on many levels because we were doing it too. We made things fun, did it as a family, kept out of blame, shame or guilt (know that as a mom this was a continual process for me), enjoyed the lessons as much as possible, and now we have many great memories of this time period, surprisingly.

This is part of Kaiya's autobiography she wrote for an autobiography assignment in fourth grade about our time in Spain.

When I was 8, I went to Spain, Europe. I had a lot of fun. I went to the Rock of Gibraltar, which is in Africa. It was a 20 minute drive from where we were in Spain. At night we would go walk down on the beach, and once we built a teepee out of Bamboo, logs, twigs, rope, seaweed and rocks. Once we went to a zoo in Spain. It was called Sellwoo Zoo. It was a lot of fun. I got to hold a full grown Anaconda, and we went to a snake show!!! In the morning at the hotel my family would go to the buffet. – Kaiya Rayvin Francis

The interesting part about this autobiography for me is that it does not highlight any of the treatments we did while we were in Spain. She never talks about the four hours a day we were in the clinic, the supplements we took, or the blood and urine we had taken regularly. In our focus being on the fun things we did, her focus was also on that. Our belief that this would be a learning experience and fun transcended to her experience and her memories, stories and beliefs created from this time period.

My outcome/result in all of this was not only to treat and prevent her tumor from coming back but also to empower her and our family through the process, build all of our bodies into a healthier state than they were before this happened and learn and grow as much as possible while having fun. Ultimately, I knew that creating an empowering experience would allow my daughter, myself and my family to not retain any facet of trauma from this experience.

CHAPTER 3

THE ULTIMATE LACK OF EMPOWERMENT: GENERATIONAL PARENTAL DISEMPOWERMENT AND TRAUMA

"This is the part where I break free."
– Ariana Grande

Generational disempowerment is when parents, grandparents or other extended generational lineage have disempowering beliefs that transfer to the present individual. These beliefs exist in reality for the initial person holding them but are transferred to the next generation without anyone having any knowledge or awareness. These beliefs can either be transferred in thought, word or physiology. This disenables the person to know or understand where, when or why these belief patterns exist and/or sometimes even how they got there. These belief patterns, which manifest into behavior patterns, exist unconsciously and may be transferred overtly or covertly depending on whether they are spoken or inferred. A specific example of generational parental disempowerment exists fully within my own lineage.

My great-grandmother was a woman who lived during the depression. In that she had to make money and find a way to feed her family, my sense is she was desperate when she decided to prostitute my grandmother as a little girl in order to make money to feed the family. My grandmother, in turn, developed an internal hatred and rage toward others because of this and an altered sense of reality with respect to sexual abuse. My mother, in turn, was sexually abused when she was young and subject to many covert beliefs around sex and safety as well as being subject to many behavior patterns around anger and rage. Not surprisingly, I was date raped when I was 16 and have had to work hard to overcome patterns of anger and rage that I had turned inward on myself when I was younger.

The universal divinity for me, however, is that I have been fortunate enough to turn my generational disempowerment into empowerment for myself and others in choosing and working within my professional career. Over the last 20 years in my private practice, I have had the privilege of working with many clients that have been raped and/or been the product of sexual abuse and have learned consciously or unconsciously to turn their anger and hatred toward themselves as well. My own experience and healing through many facets of growth enable me to sit empathically with these clients as they heal. I am truly honored that I have been able to use my experiences and the experiences of my lineage to help heal others.

Another example of generational parental disempowerment is displayed in my practice as well. A large percentage of my clients with eating disorders have parents who have rigid beliefs about food, weight and exercise. Their parents may exercise 2-3 hours per day, eat only "low" calorie foods and/or criticize their bodies in the mirror tirelessly. The child, adopting these beliefs, feels like this is the "right" way to eat, exercise or feel about their body. Their father's or mother's beliefs about food, weight, body image and exercise become their own. The difference for my clients, however, is that they may be more extreme in their behaviors or viewed as being more extreme by their family and obtain a diagnosis of an eating disorder.

Breaking generational disempowerment is essential for everyone but definitely a necessary component of treatment for clients with an eating disorder. Discovering their own internal beliefs regarding these parts of their life allows my clients to see what beliefs are their own and what beliefs are their parents. Doing this allows my clients to identify what beliefs THEY want to have around food, exercise and weight. Allowing my clients to see that this started as their parents' beliefs as opposed to their own is a key component of their healing. This ultimately leads to them being able to define their choices with their own outcome/result in mind based on themselves and how they actually want to eat.

In turn, I also work with women and men who have stopped taking care of themselves physically, mentally and emotionally as they have become parents due to generational disempowerment. Having parents who did not have self-care principles or who shunned others for having self-care principles shows up regularly for another facet of my clientele. Looking at one's own belief construct with respect to self-care and determining your own vision, instead of your parents' or grandparents', is essential in breaking free from generational parent empowerment.

The Ultimate Lack of Empowerment : Trauma - Are You Recreating or Renegotiating the Past?

Over the years, trauma has been looked at in many different ways, some complex and some markedly simple. In taking a two-year specialty training in trauma, I realized that the definition of trauma is markedly simple but the treatment can be complex, depending realistically on the individual. The definition of trauma *is anything that changes your perception of the world.* It is that simple.

Obviously there are various degrees or levels of trauma and that is what leads to the complexity and differences in treatment. However, in reality, an intense fall on a bike that truly keeps a child in fear of riding again is trauma just as a rape is an identified trauma. The differences and intensity of renegotiating this trauma would be radically different. However, some of the core underlying beliefs and emotions would present as the same.

All trauma creates a feeling of overwhelm. There is no choice in trauma, and no focus on result or outcome. This can create both overwhelm in someone's body or overwhelm in someone's mind or a combination of both. This overwhelm not only creates symptoms of its own but also creates individuals' beliefs about themselves or about the world in general. Grief that is "stuck" and has not been released emotionally or physically can also create trauma. I will speak more about grief briefly in a later section.

According to Dr. Peter Levine, one of the foremost experts on trauma, the symptoms of trauma include:

- Hyperarousal
- Constriction
- Disassociation
- Feelings of helplessness
- Hypervigilance (being "on guard" at all times)
- Intrusive imagery or flashbacks

- Extreme sensitivity to light and sound
- Hyperactivity
- Exaggerated emotions and startle response
- Nightmares and night terrors
- Abrupt mood swings
- Reduced ability to deal with stress
- Difficulty sleeping

As I mentioned, treatment or renegotiation of trauma varies depending on the individual and the degree of trauma. However, the most imperative parts of renegotiation in trauma are in grounding, orienting and integrating. In a traumatic event, disorienting occurs and hypervigilance prevails. Everything is viewed as a threat. The entire central nervous system moves into fight-or-flight reactions and emotional stability follows accordingly.

> Karen, one of my young clients with anorexia, came into my office for an initial appointment after she had lost 20 pounds over the course of 5 months. Her parents, physician and therapist were radically concerned. In our initial appointment in speaking about the feelings about her food, she stated, "It's always there, everyone is always talking about it or putting it in front of me. I just stare at it when they put it down in front of me. Don't they know what it will do to me? It will make me FAT." When I asked her how does FAT feel she responded, "Like the worst thing that can ever happen to me. I would rather be dead than be fat."

In these responses you can see how individuals with eating disorders view their food and sometimes the people around them. Food is the ultimate threat to their anorexia's survival.

In learning how to ground and orient, a client can begin to learn and know their position between themselves and their environment.

In trauma and subsequent overwhelm the body and the mind hyper focus on the threat, similar to what animals do when they feel threatened in the wild. In this process, our bodies, particularly our eyes, heads, necks and minds, become constricted, frozen. This leads to disorientation and hyper focus that prevails all the time. This is called hypervigilance.

Orienting is the process of allowing the body and subsequently the mind to focus on all areas within our panoramic view in overwhelm, allowing ourselves to move our eyes, head and neck smoothly and slowly to obtain all the information in our panoramic view. As trauma disconnects us from our world, orienting reconnects us. For my client Karen, what we began with was learning about grounding and orienting to allow her to reconnect to her world without the constriction and hypervigilance.

Disassociation occurs in trauma as well. A feeling of floating above the body or not being with your body is a normal, natural response to the overwhelm. Using simple grounding techniques like breathing, body scanning and visualization can all enable disassociation to disappear and reconnect clients to the present moment.

> *Claire, a compulsive overeater I worked with for some time, described her massive binges in detail with respect to the food but when asked how she felt during these binges she said, "It's strange, it's like I am not even there. Like I am watching from another part of the room but I can't feel anything. Like someone else has taken over and I'm not home."*

For Claire, one of our first steps in treatment was teaching her how to ground herself to associate to the experience. Although connecting with herself in these large binges was not comfortable for her, I knew that without connection there is no ability to change. It is like trying to help someone on the other side of the world without connecting to them in any way. You cannot change behavior until you connect to yourself while you are in the behavior. Ultimately, then you can sit in choice around that behavior, leading to ultimate empowerment.

Without connection to behavior, re-enactment of trauma can occur. Re-enactment occurs when someone is unable to transform their trauma. It occurs because the victim of overwhelm has not been able to complete their feeling of energy discharge in their body and free their mind of negative belief patterns. Therefore, re-enactment can occur externally in behavior or internally in thought patterns or more likely a combination of both. This not only compounds the trauma in the client's mind and body but also increases their feeling of helplessness.

> Riley, a client of mine with bulimia, had been raped by a family member repeatedly when she was growing up. The traumatic facet of her bulimia was a recapitulation of her beliefs about herself based on these molestations. Her purges were invasive, abusive and punitive. She also put herself in dangerous situations sexually.
>
> I received a phone call from her one day sobbing after she had been to the rape crisis unit in our area. She had agreed to meet, at his house, a man that she had only spoken to on the phone with. As she drove over there, she had a "bad" feeling but "pushed" through it and

ignored it (so often victims of trauma are not connected to their intuition or ignore it or push through it as they had done and had to do in the abuse cycle). When she knocked and walked into his house he jumped out from behind the door, grabbed her, dragged her inside and raped her repeatedly.

This is a prime example of re-enactment—being or placing yourself in situations consciously or unconsciously that allow you to re-enact the trauma of origin. For the majority of clients, re-enactment occurs unconsciously. It can be worked with and worked through with the right practitioner who works with and specializes in trauma. In learning how to renegotiate the trauma, new understandings and beliefs can be formed.

Three years later, after working extensively through these issues, Riley truly understood her beliefs and meanings around herself and her re-enactment. She ultimately worked on various parts of herself and healing. During this process, she found an amazing partner who loved and supported her through her learning. She stopped purging completely, started eating healthy/nurturing food, began to focus on healthy habit, sexual intimacy and became empowered professionally. To date, she is completely free from her eating disorder and lives with this same partner in a healthy, intimate relationship.

Honestly, as a practitioner, I always hold the belief that a client can heal NO MATTER WHAT the circumstances they have been given. I hold this belief in order to keep myself focused and in an empowered state even if the client is not.

Holding the belief that a client will prevail over his/her circumstance is essential for success. This previous client is one that I can honestly say allows me to absolutely know without a doubt that all individuals can heal. She not only healed herself but has achieved empowerment in many facets of her life that were ultimately wounded.

As a practitioner, holding the belief that a client will heal and be whole is an extremely important key to their success. It allows both you and the client to trust the process and, I believe, enables you both to trust each other on an even greater level. As a practitioner, believing that the client will heal and achieve whatever they desire gives the client something they may not have ever received as well, unconditional support. This, in and of itself, can provide an immense amount of healing.

CHAPTER 4

DECONSTRUCTING THE BELIEF CODE: IDENTIFYING AND UNDERSTANDING YOUR BELIEFS AND HOW THEY AFFECT YOUR ABILITY TO CONNECT TO YOUR TRUE SELF

> "Beliefs have the power to create and the power to destroy. Human beings have the awesome ability to take any experience of their lives and create a meaning that disempowers them or one that can literally save their lives."
> – Tony Robbins

A belief is an idea one accepts as being true or real. Beliefs are created during significant time periods in our life. Childhood, trauma, difficult times and grief/loss are all time periods of significance in which beliefs are created. The stories of our lives truly hold the beliefs we create. Beliefs in ourselves or others truly create the perception of reality in our world. Our stories create our beliefs and from our beliefs we create the meanings that surround our world.

Beliefs exist in everyone's conscious and unconscious. Yet, for the majority of people I have worked with they do not even know what a belief is or how they are impacted by their own beliefs. Beliefs exist in the deep crevices in our mind and dictate and control our emotions, behaviors and feelings in our bodies, yet most of us never know what they are or how they came into existence. Identifying your own beliefs is the first step in the process of deconstruction and can ultimately lead to freedom from disempowering beliefs. Please see the final chapter for tools to identify your own or your clients' beliefs.

Throughout the last 20 years of my practice, I have identified various types of beliefs. These types of beliefs include:

- Others' beliefs we take on as our own (this could be beliefs of the media, culture or friends)
- Generational beliefs
- Old beliefs created during significant periods in the past
- Limiting beliefs
- Negative beliefs
- Global beliefs
- Core beliefs
- True beliefs

As we are raised in childhood, we are significantly influenced by the beliefs that are held by the people that surround us. I spoke of generational parental disempowerment earlier in this book. However, other beliefs that influence us can also encompass social beliefs, media beliefs, cultural beliefs and peer beliefs. Adolescents believing their body needs to look a certain way may be holding a media or cultural belief in our society. Symmetrically, a woman who believes she can't work and be a great mother may be responding to her cultural or peer beliefs as well.

For young children, this may mean parents or other caregivers and as we get into adolescence it may be equated more to our peers or social media influences. These beliefs may become our own beliefs as we are taught to take them from those around us either to fit in or to feel loved. For example, if a parent believes that children should be seen and not heard they will:

1. Treat the child accordingly, meaning they will expect behavior that is in accordance with their belief. Punishments or play will be dictated according to this belief. This could be defined as a covert belief infliction since the belief is not imparted consciously but is imparted in behavior patterns.
2. The parent(s) may also repeat this belief regularly, thus inflicting this belief on a cognitive level to the child. This could be defined as an overt belief infliction since the belief is stated in plain, cognitive terms.

Another type of belief construct are old beliefs. Old beliefs are beliefs we create during significant time periods. During significant time periods we create beliefs to provide some facet of meaning surrounding an event. This may be done consciously, but more likely done unconsciously. Creating beliefs without intention significantly hinders your life and as life progresses and these beliefs are not changed they radically impact your present and future. Significant time periods would include times of loss, trauma and other significant events.

A prime example of an old belief would be a mother who has a sick child developing a belief that she is solely responsible for keeping her child healthy, feeling a burden of responsibility. As her child becomes healthier she may then try to control her child in other ways to protect the child from illness. The mother may move into over-control patterns and hypervigilance based on this belief pattern. Conversely, an adolescent who believes that eating carbohydrates will make her fat will need to change this belief construct in order to fully recover from his/her eating disorder.

Limiting beliefs are beliefs we have created in the past that limit us in our thoughts, actions, emotions or behaviors. They hinder us from truly finding our destiny and limit us ultimately from connecting with ourselves and others in the way we were designed to do. Thinking that in order to have a lot of money you must be selfish is a prime example of a limiting belief.

Negative beliefs are similar in their enactment but truly only reflect negative components about oneself. Negative beliefs may be stated in "I am" terms which impact a person's identity and core infrastructure. "I am too much for others to handle," "I am selfish," "I am fat." Negative beliefs transform and transcend how people view themselves and how they act in the world in their behavior patterns. For the person who believes they are selfish, they may give constantly to others and never give to themselves, enacting the opposite of their belief. For the person that believes they are fat, they may try to keep their body and food at a certain weight and/or food calorie intake or expenditure. These negative beliefs dictate and drive not only how they feel about themselves but also determine their behaviors as well.

Core beliefs are very similar to negative beliefs in that they are always stated in "I am" terms. Core beliefs are the very essence of how we see ourselves, other people, the world or our future. The difference with core beliefs is that they are not always stated in the negative or impact feelings or behavior negatively. Core beliefs are beliefs about ourselves that provide our infrastructure, the structure of our personality, behaviors and emotional tenacity. They dictate who and how we will be in connection with others and in connection with ourselves. A core belief can be anything from "I am a good listener" to "I am depressed." They truly are our labels for ourselves and our identity structure.

Conversely, global beliefs are beliefs we hold about the world globally. For example, "All women need a good man" or "All men are jerks." These beliefs are the lenses in our glasses that show us how we see the world. They dictate and determine how we act in the world and how we feel about the world as a whole.

Any type of belief we hold that we criticize, condemn or judge takes the energy, even in this negative fashion, to ignite and expand it. Negative energy expands things just as positive energy does and it's worth noting that this impact affects our beliefs as well. In trying to change a belief pattern, it is important NOT to judge, criticize or condemn it as it will only ignite this belief and others linked to this belief.

The last type of beliefs are a bit more difficult to find but definitely do exist. We do truly have beliefs that, once identified, we own and want to own. These beliefs serve us. They move us into being who we are destined to be. They allow us to truly be who we are and they serve not only ourselves but the world for greater good. They may be a core belief or a global belief but inevitably they always protect, preserve and persist in a positive facet of one's life.

The day after Christmas, my daughter, Kaiya, was crying because she did not want our Christmas elves to leave. She felt like she wouldn't believe in them next year and wanted to hold onto them as long as she could. After lots of tears and a bit of laughter, I started to talk to her about beliefs. "Kaiya," I said, "no one can ever make you change your beliefs about anything, even your belief about the elves being real. When people don't believe in Santa or their Christmas elves anymore, it is because they make that choice to not believe. No one can change the beliefs you want to hold onto. Those beliefs are yours, they're real for you and they make Christmas magic for you. Those are the beliefs you keep, the ones you choose and the ones that add magic to your life and those around you."

A Case Study of Beliefs – Kaiya's Story

After Kaiya, my daughter, who was at the time six years old, went into the hospital for what we thought was appendicitis and came out with one tumor and one fallopian tube removed, my beliefs around health, safety and mothering shifted radically. I remember the moment the surgeon took us back into a "separate room" right after her surgery. My husband and I were sitting there waiting for what we thought would be a quick, easy surgery for her "appendicitis." The surgeon came into the waiting room and asked that we go back to a separate room to speak. Now, I have spent a bit of time in the hospital in internships and with sick family members and I know that being asked to go to a separate room to speak is not for good news. So immediately my stomach began to get queasy, my legs felt like jello and my ears started to ring. Everything stood still for a moment.

When my husband, I and the surgeon went back to the room to speak the surgeon said, "Well, Mr. and Mrs.

Francis, the good news is that your daughter does not have appendicitis." I stopped breathing at this point; I knew there was a pervasive "but" coming to this sentence. My head was swimming, my heart was racing.

"After we went in with a microscopic camera to get a look at her appendix we found a tumor the size of a lemon hanging from her fallopian tube. It had twisted upon itself and infarcted (killed itself). That was why she was running fevers and in so much pain."

Immediately I held onto my stomach, where I was eight months pregnant with my third child, and thought, *She lost a fallopian tube? Will she be able to have babies? Tumor? What tumor?* So many questions prevailed. Fear, anxiety and grief all came into the room, surrounding me, I couldn't breathe. I couldn't think.

I heard my husband say, "Is it cancerous?"

The surgeon replied, "We are not sure, we have sent it to our lab to start testing."

All I kept thinking was she won't be able to have children. So I asked, "Will she be able to have children?" The ironic part about this question is that I have been educated both on an undergraduate and graduate level on anatomy/physiology and am a woman myself so you would really think I would have known the answer to that. That's the infinite wisdom of shock; there is no memory, no instance of holding what you know.

The surgeon said, kindly, "Yes, Mrs. Francis, as you know you have two fallopian tubes. She will be just fine in that area. We do, however, need you to schedule an appointment with pediatric oncology in the next week so we can begin discussing her options for treatment."

I thought to myself, Oncology!!! Huh? That is cancer! What cancer! Oh my god, cancer, cancer, cancer!! They think she has cancer! CANCER—WHAT!!! Fear came into my world and left me breathless. Fear crept in and survival mode took a front seat. For the next four days I slept, or rather lay, next to my six-year-old little girl in the hospital while she recovered with my eight-month-old sleeping in my womb. The nurses in the pediatric ward were amazing to me, constantly bringing in extra pillows or skipping nighttime checks upon my request so we could both get some rest.

Rest, for me, but not sleep. My mind started working, clinically. My husband and I jumped into practitioner mode. We needed to figure this out. How did this happen to our girl? I would review and re-review her labs every day and text them to my husband. He would search voraciously on the internet and call any and all the connections we had that could give us some insight. We took this on as our responsibility. We both have education in treatment and prevention of disease, in particular cancer, and we were going to use it. In the hospital, our beliefs held fast—we both knew and believed that it was mainly our responsibility to figure this out and fix it. The empowerment was amazing but I will say the responsibility in it was deafening.

Once we got home, we continued this journey of discovering and uncovering what this was and how it got there. The medical community did their part as well, trying to figure out what type of tumor it was and why it was there. Splices of her tumor were sent off to three prevalent medical facilities in and outside of the United States. All three of these facilities pronounced their inability to determine whether or not the tumor was malignant or benign. My daughter, apparently, was an anomaly. She was a true medical case study, being studied and later to be reported on and in medical journals.

As I was home trying to figure my way through this, I came upon many people in my community that held their own beliefs. They expressed that I was either

1. *"Off my rocker." Just let the doctors handle it, they know what they are doing.*
2. *"To blame." What have you been feeding her? Maybe you should have been stricter with her diet? It's so sad, you could have prevented this with all you know. Maybe you should have adjusted her more. Are you drinking alkaline water? Are you doing the healing diet? You are going change everything now, aren't you?*

Now for me, personally, it was easy to dispel others who believed number one. I am, in fact, a bit of a rebel in nature and do not always find it a negative to "go against the grain." But for those who chimed in with belief number two, it ignited a fuel under a fire that had been a burning default belief for years. A default belief is a belief we fall back to when we are extremely tired, radically stressed or experiencing grief, loss or trauma. "I am the responsible one." I took this belief and set it on fire. Fear and responsibility crept in together. "What if something I did caused this?" "I wasn't a good enough mom." At the core, "I am not good enough" and "I have to do everything" combined and ignited with fear as its fire. Underneath, grief prevailed and I did not even recognize it. Life took over for a few months at this time.

Our dear friend and office manager passed away from lung cancer on April first. Six days later my third son was born.

My pursuit of how, why and what I could do with and for my daughter came to a poetic pause as I took care of my newborn, which, quite frankly, I look at as a godsend, truly, it allowed me to step back for a bit. I realized throughout that summer that holding these beliefs and functioning from this place of fear, worry and responsibility would not allow me to prevail during this time and around her cancer. The doctors had found no answers as to how or why this tumor existed or if it would ever come back again. The pediatric oncologist could only tell us that the best they could offer us was to do CT scans every six months for the next 10 years to see if it would come back during puberty. This was unacceptable to both me and my husband.

As I caught my breath emotionally and physically as my third little guy got older, I remember beginning to design how I could get through this, find answers, get treatment, prevent anything else from happening and allow our whole family to prevail and get healthier during this process. In the past, I had always believed that everything I had gone through would always be used to help others grow, heal and understand things. I needed to go back to that. I was clinically trained as a dietitian and could understand all of her nutrition needs and medically interpret all of her labs. We could make radical movement on her nutrition and physiological health and with my husband's background as a chiropractor and preventative disease specialist we could combine our forces to attack this. I found gratitude.

Through my gratitude and movement of my grief, I found my new belief, which was a recreation of my old one: "I am a conduit for healing. Everything I learn during this process will one day be given through me to others to help them or their loved ones heal." I checked this new belief out physiologically and emotionally. I felt revived, refreshed, energized. I visualized what this belief would look like. I planned what I would need to do to prevail during this time to learn as much as possible and to grow in every way imaginable as a mother, woman, practitioner and professional. I dove in! I felt strong, resilient. Having my new belief, emotional way, visual and plan enabled me to begin a two-year journey of infinite possibility of learning and growth. It enabled me to ask myself questions that opened up awesome possibilities for healing for my daughter and myself.

Ultimately it also opened me up to another belief I crafted during this time to enable me to physically sustain myself in the lack of sleep that I had to get to complete the tasks I needed to. "I will sleep when I am dead." That may seem a bit odd, but for me it allowed to really engage in the aliveness of life and motivate me to wake up at 4:30 a.m. to start my day every day. I absolutely know that without this I would not have been able to go through that journey and come out on the other side.

As a practitioner, I know that there are two types of motivators that move people to action: "moving away from pain motivators" and "moving toward pleasure motivators." In my experience we individually are motivated by one or the other and this is specifically different person to person. Understanding whether or not you move into action based on these facets can transform how you motivate yourself and your clients.

I am a "moving toward" person and function much better as I move toward something that will give me or someone in my life pleasure or healing. In creating my new belief it allowed me to be energized in "moving toward" positive things, which moved me in radical action. Creating beliefs that align with you or your clients' motivation strategy is imperative to move clients into action.

An Aside about Grief—Grief Redefined

As it is a normal reaction to the diagnosis of a chronic or acute illness, the emotion of grief becomes pervasive. In its nature, however, grief is not always identified or dealt with. Even for my clients who have anorexia or bulimia, the feelings of loss and grief prevail for the parents but are never identified or healed. Truly defined, GRIEF is a LOSS. Truth be told, this loss can be around anything, your children's, your family's or your own health, your marriage, your job or anything else that creates the sense or feeling of loss. Grief is not just about someone dying, it is about suffering the feeling of a loss. Redefined, we can see that grief is around us more than we realize or identify and is radically under-identified.

Grief, in itself, is a moveable emotion, easy to work with once identified. In fact, research has proven that people who have healed even the most intense grief come out on the other side of this grief with more resiliency and strength, and they prevail much more than individuals that don't. Grief, in its healing, can actually make us stronger, more grateful and more connected to ourselves and others. Grief healed is transformative, grief that has not been healed and is stuck presents as trauma. It can even present as post-traumatic stress disorder, or PTSD, on psychological testing.

Trauma or stuck grief radically shifts a person's belief system, impacting major areas of their life, and those around them. For example, a man who loses his job and pushes through his grief to find a job immediately may show signs of hypervigilance or anxiety or hypovigilance or depression and begin to believe that he will never be able to find a job again. This may turn into a more global belief and he may even believe that he can't do anything right. A woman who has a miscarriage may begin to believe that she was not meant to have children, or even worse that she wasn't meant to be a mother at all.

If I had thought back through this more when my daughter was first diagnosed I would not have had those months of spiraling. It would have enabled me to cut down my time in the beginning of spinning emotionally. Hitting grief head on allows you to truly understand, feel, own and overcome or overthrow it.

Before I got pregnant with my daughter, I had a miscarriage. During this experience I learned valuable tools to help with my own grief. I have taught clients and friends about this and have allowed them to radically decrease their time in healing as well. I have also recently been certified as a grief coach and have continued to craft these steps in my learning.

> The prerequisite to this seven-step process is to actually "hire" a support group to help you enact these steps as needed. Ask your spouse and/or one of two of your closest friends to support you during this time and this process or actually hire a professional to support and assist you with this. For me, I had my husband and two close friends support me. I was actually blessed in the fact that one of those friends is a very prestigious therapist. She was

actually the person who called me every few hours for two days and the other friend actually came over for a few hours one evening. You don't need a friend who is a therapist, though. You can ask a friend, family member or spouse to do any role that you need to help in your healing.

The Seven Steps to Overthrow Grief

1. Make space to grieve. Find a space you will be through this time, your house, a hotel room or someone else's house.
2. Take time to grieve. In a world where we go through everything fast, emotions are the one thing that won't listen to our fast-paced life. Grief needs time to heal. Take some days off work or off life to be with your feelings. This will allow you to actually heal the grief instead of letting it become stuck. Stuck grief, presenting as PTSD, can destroy your life and those around you. Trust me, it will make things a whole lot easier in your world in the long run.
3. Be present in your grief. Just be with it. Emotions aren't emergencies and grief won't kill you. Let yourself be present in the feeling and stay away from distractions. This sounds easy but may actually present as the hardest step as we are so trained in our society to distract from "bad" feelings. Staying present are easy words to say but not necessarily an easy skill to master.
4. Ask for and be intentional in what you need for support. This is what the support team is for; use it to provide a healing space for you.
5. Now here is the "to do" part. Every hour on the hour, if not more, ask yourself, "What do I want to do to feel

loved or nurtured now?" Then actually give yourself an answer. Do you need to lie down and relax? Do you need to cry? Do you need a good meal? Do you need to sit outside with the sunshine on your face? Enlist one of your support team to call you every few hours to give you connection to the outside world, bring you food or offer you anything else you might need. Ask for what you need from yourself and your support team. This truly allows your heart and head to heal. It slows things down, nurtures you, supports the process and enables you to come out the other side of grief, healed.

6. Once you get an answer that connects you back to the world you will know you are through the majority of the process. For me, it was on the third day. When I asked myself "What do I need," I replied, "I want to call my clients and get my schedule intact for next week." I was ready to go back into the world.

7. Before you return fully, take a few moments and reflect upon the gifts that this lesson in life has taught you. Journal, write or vision these gifts. What have you learned? What can you bring new into the world after having this experience? What are the gifts you have and what are the gifts you can give to others after this experience? This process allows you to return and rewrite any beliefs that have been altered. It allows you to connect back into your core, your heart center, and find the space that has healed. This process will allow you to access and expand this space to allow connection to yourself in your healing and expansion to create the miraculous beauty that comes after the storm.

Be courageous in your vulnerability. It is the one way through grief. After my miscarriage, I did this process for three days. I cried, rested, sat in the sun, and ate good food. After three days I laughed, I went for a walk and felt joy again. I have never felt any regret, grief or sadness regarding that miscarriage. I believe at my core that it was my body and soul getting ready to bring forth my daughter. I have no negative, stuck beliefs, fear or anger around this experience, just love, light and joy. Joy in the fact that it allowed me to learn more about life and joy in the fact that I can now relate to other women who have had a miscarriage. Joy in learning and knowing more about the process of healing.

Every person I have told this to has used this process for different amounts of time and in different circumstances. But all report the same thing. It is amazing how quickly emotions shift and move if you give them space, time and presence.

Grief that is unhealed not only diminishes or destroys our own existence but it can also diminish or destroy marriages as well. My best friend in life and soul sister had a baby with Down's syndrome over 13 years ago. In their situation, they did not know that their child was going to be born with "the extra," as they now call it (referring to the extra gene that individuals with Down's syndrome have). Truly, however, in knowing my niece I absolutely believe that the people that are born with "the extra" really are special and both my friend and her husband believe and have experienced the joy she has brought into their lives.

However, for the first many months the amount of grief that my friend and her husband experienced was astounding. Life as they had known it would never be the same. The life they thought they would have after the birth of their child was lost. This was a process of releasing the vision of what was and embracing the joy in the "what is." It can be part of many phases of life from birth to death to the loss of a job to divorce or other challenges that fall into this broad category.

On top of their grief, they had lifestyle changes, health challenges and emotional issues they had to overcome. All of this compounded not only on themselves individually but also on their marriage. The statistics for couples that divorce with children with special needs is astounding. Even more interesting to me and disheartening is the fact that no one in the hospital then or since has spoken to them about grief or the process of healing grief. Remember, grief is not only specifically about a person dying. Grief is defined as a loss of who or what you thought was meant to be.

There are actually steps to help those you know going through grief. In your initial conversation with the person:

First: Acknowledge the person who is grieving, make eye contact, breath and mirror their body language.
Second: Listen and be present with them in their grief without fixing them. Let them be in their own experience without jumping in to fix the problem or the emotion. So often we lose our presence with an individual when we try to change or fix their emotion. Presence encompasses a profound healing in grief and should not be overlooked.
Third: Give hope and encouragement around their situation. Be specific on how you will or want to help. Don't ask, "What can I do for you?" Ask specifically, "What is one thing I can do for you and your family?" Once you have done this one thing then ask for one more. Individuals in grief have a difficult time making any more decisions than they need to. By asking them to decide on one more thing, even if it is how to help, can even be a bit too much. Ask them to give you one thing to help with at a time and allow them the freedom to change or add as they need to.

Fourth: Use your heart to speak instead of your head. Be vulnerable and allow yourself to be real and honest in your communication.

Good things to say to someone grieving:
You're not alone—you have a support team and I am on it.
I don't know what to say.
I can't imagine how you feel.
My heart is with you.

Aurora Winters is a foremost expert on grief and growth through grief. You can find more extensive resources about grief by accessing her website at **www.aurorawinter.com** or from her book *From Heartbreak to Happiness*.

You can also help the person grieving by referring back to what life was like prior to their loss. "What was your favorite thing about..." What was your life like before the divorce happened..." Subsequently, then link it to their present and future. "What will you keep with you forever, in your heart or in your world?" "How will you bring that into the future to help yourself or others?"

Allow this to fully expand for an individual as it is ready. Some are ready to make the link fairly quickly after the loss and some need to heal a bit and stay in the emotion for longer. Know that each person goes through this process in their own way and in their own time.

In order to fully understand the difference between trauma and grief I have used Dr. Peter Levine and Maggie Kline's definition listed in *Trauma Through a Child's Eyes*. Note some of the simplistic, yet radical differences between grief and trauma and also how they can be related.

Grief	**Trauma**
Generalized reaction is sadness	Generalized reaction is terror
Talking can be a relief	Talking can be difficult or impossible
Generally does NOT Impact our self-	Generally, impacts our self-image and confidence image or confidence negatively in a negative way
Anger is non-violent	Anger can become violent to self or others
Reactions stand alone	May include grief reactions

"The only limits you have are the limits you believe."
-Wayne Dwyer

CHAPTER 5

THE LINK BETWEEN BELIEFS AND EMOTIONS

> "It's not the decisions we make in life, it is our feelings about those decisions."
> – Wendi Francis

The first part in understanding our beliefs is identifying the ones we have. As a practitioner, I use a client's language, model of the world and physiology to identify their beliefs. I look for patterns of language and thought that create these beliefs. Words and phrases such as "I am," "I should," "I can't," "everybody," "always," "somebody" and "nobody" are all parts of a belief construct.

Emotions are created by a part of the brain called the amygdala, or the midbrain, and they respond directly to the beliefs we create in our mind. Emotions are things we feel, and some of us think about, all day long but rarely do we understand where they come from or how they got there. Emotions do not exist alone; they are supported by the things we focus on, say to ourselves and store in our body, the table of our state mentioned earlier.

Emotions are created and stem from the beliefs we hold that we create from our story about the events that happened. So, in essence...

STORY ---BELIEFS---EMOTIONS

The story that we hold around a process of events is the beginning of what creates our beliefs. Even during a process of events, I have seen each individual going through these events to hold different stories. When asking my clients what they remember around certain things in their childhood, their stories inevitably vary from their parents' and sometimes even their siblings. The beliefs they hold from these stories clearly differ as well.

There are various techniques for practitioners to help clients craft new stories to allow them to begin the healing process. Neuro-Linguistic Programming, Somatic Experiencing and various other modalities use differing techniques to help clients work through and heal their stories. I highlight some of these in the back section of this book.

Ultimately, however, the most empowering part of this is that you can actually change your belief without crafting or renegotiating the story. Asking yourself or your client, "What belief do you want to have?" or "What belief would have allowed you to come through that experience in the way you would have wanted to?" or "What belief would allow you to live and have the life you would want to now?" Enabling clients to see that they have a choice in the beliefs they hold and the beliefs they create, empowers them in knowing that life is about action versus reaction. It lets them know that they have a say, a voice and a CHOICE and can determine their own destiny instead of it being in the hands of others.

Sandy, a client who was an overeater, came to her first session telling me a story of when she was a little girl. "When I was seven I remember my mom bringing me to my doctor and him telling her, and I, that I was too big for my height and that my mom needed to put me on a diet. My mom agreed, emphatically, and wanted me to lose weight as well. I remember feeling so unacceptable and ashamed. I went home and cried while my mom talked to me about how I would only be allowed to eat 'these' certain foods that she had labeled in the house and that I would start to have exercise after school.

"That was the first of a long history of diets I have been on. I truly believe that my body does not work and that I have no willpower. I am weak and don't deserve anything good that comes into my live. I feel so ashamed. I will never be able to be skinny."

Our work began that day. We first looked at her story of being young and put on a diet and what that meant for her body, physiologically, and her emotions, mentally. We dove in together to understand and heal the story. The next and most important part of our work began in discovering her beliefs that came from this story.

In writing down a client's language, I can very quickly see in black and white what their beliefs are. Depending on the client, I may also use some insight on their body language. For Sandy, her beliefs centered around her body not working, her willpower and her weakness.

These beliefs, in turn, radically affected her emotions or feelings about herself. If her belief had been that she could do anything she set her mind to with food or that she could overcome her eating addiction with the proper tools she would have felt strong, self-centered and focused. If she completely trusted her body, metabolically, she would know that it would know what to do with the food she gave it. If she trusted herself with food, she would identify deserving goodness, even greatness. Her beliefs disenabled her to feel emotionally strong in her actions and in her body.

Just by looking at our initial dialogue can you see what beliefs she held? Her beliefs included but were not limited to her body not working, her having no willpower, her being weak, her being undeserving, and her never being able to be skinny. Not to mention more we uncovered in our work together. In this her brain linked these beliefs to various emotions that continued to keep her feeling stuck in these beliefs without refuge.

Beliefs and the Brain

Beliefs affect our emotions which ultimately are located primarily in the middle brain. The frontal brain is called the cortex or thinking brain. This is the part of the brain that we use to analyze, manipulate and understand data. It is only responsible for creating and holding 20% of our information we use to change. The rest of the brain holds all of our wisdom that helps us to change. That is why words such as beliefs that effect the mid and back brain are so important in how we think, feel and act.

The back brain or primal brain, is where we store primal reactions. This part of the brain is known as our "reptilian" brain as it holds the parts of our thinking and feeling that is most closely related to the animal kingdom. Processes such as breathing, digestion, circulation, elimination, temperature regulation, fight-or-flight response and movement are completed via this section of the brain. The midbrain is the part of the brain that controls the majority of our emotional states.

With intense emotions such as anxiety, fear and shame, the amygdala shuts down and puts your brain in "survival mode," only allowing small bits of information to get through to the frontal cortex. These emotions instigate the amygdala to use excess oxygen and nutrients as well. This need for increased oxygen is truly why deep breathing or breathing techniques help to calm these emotions.

When the amygdala shuts down the prefrontal cortex due to excessive negative emotions, the person cannot process new or even stored information. Teaching someone in these emotional states (anxiety, fear or shame) will not be received. It is interesting to note here that the majority of my clients' parents who brought them to me for nutrition therapy always wanted them to "be educated" and get a "meal plan." This I knew in reality could not be accomplished based on the amygdala system of input I just explained. Trust, grounding and orienting all need to be accomplished before education can take place.

Once the brain is ready to receive new information, like a new belief system, it is important to note the hippocampus role in this. The hippocampus is right next to the amygdala and it is where new sensory input is linked to both previously stored memories and previously learned knowledge. Once these links are made, practicing these new beliefs will allow this part of the brain to continue to practice those links, actually forming new synapses or bridges between these spaces in the brain.

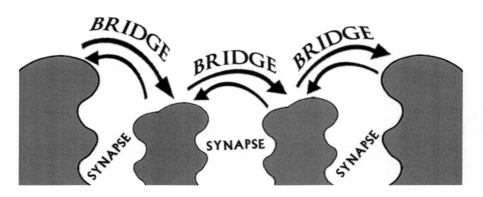

Each time you practice and review these new beliefs your brain builds new bridges to expand and continue these belief structures, linking them from the frontal cortex to the midbrain to the back brain. Even more amazing is the fact that practicing these new beliefs while doing certain activities like interacting with friends, laughing and physical activity can actually increase dopamine levels in the brain, further compounding the brain's ability to build these bridges of pleasure. THIS IS WHY ONCE A NEW BELIEF IS CREATED, PRACTICING THESE BELIEFS DURING THESE PLEASURABLE ACTIVITIES COMPOUNDS THE EXPANSION OF THESE BELIEFS REMARKABLY, ALLOWING THE BENEFIT TO TRULY HAVE A LASTING EFFECT AND CREATE ULTIMATE LASTING CHANGE.

CHAPTER 6

FEAR AND SHAME BASED BELIEFS: A SLIPPERY SLOPE

"I want to know if you can be alone with
yourself and truly like the company you keep in
the empty moments."
— Oriah Mountain Dreamer

Worth noting here is the difference that fear- and shame-based beliefs hold. Fear is an intense emotion that we feel in relation to something we feel threatened by. Fear can be real or imagined and there truly is no differential distinction between the two. In fear, the amygdala shuts down the prefrontal cortex, disenabling us from bringing in new information or rationalizing present information. This is the system that is in effect when you are home alone and you hear a noise upstairs and your brain has a difficult time rationalizing what it heard.

The truth about fear can be found in the acronym

F- False
E- Evidence
A Appearing
R- Real

Fear is the one emotion everyone runs from but it is truly the emotion that shrinks when you actually run toward it. I remember when I was young that I was afraid there was an alligator living under my bed. I was paralyzed by fear at night, and my mom would come in and pick me up and put me down on the floor so that I could actually see with my own eyes that there was no alligator under there. It was only then that I could relax and go to sleep. Confronting the fear is truly the only way through it.

Beliefs created in fear and that create fear hold the same intensity in our world. They disenable us from thinking rationally and they disempower us from creating our choices, results and outcomes. It is a spiral emotion that holds a lot of negative energy that can be transferred from one belief to the next like a frog leaping from the different lily pads of fear. Fear can construct beliefs and manipulate them to appear differently. So a belief that presents as one thing can change into something different. There may be a core belief underneath a surface belief or there may be a limiting belief on top of an identity belief. Fear creates anxiety. Anxiety is a "spiral" emotion that links beliefs and emotions together in erratic, overpowering patterns.

In working with clients with eating disorders the last 20 years, I have had a lot of experience in working with fear-based beliefs. One of the most prevalent limiting beliefs I hear in my office is "I am fat." This belief is based in fear of what they are afraid will happen if they eat. It may be something that has happened to them in the past. In truth, some of my clients actually were heavy in the past and that is why they turned to restriction and dieting to solve their issue. This was definitely the case for Carole, who came to me as a client when she was 19 years old on referral from a therapist in my area.

Carole came to my office for an initial assessment after her parents had watched her go from 120 pounds to 90 pounds. She had worked with another dietitian and therapist that contracted with her to gain back to 120 pounds, her ideal goal weight. At that point she got scared after she had dropped those 30 pounds in response to a diet she had put herself on.

In her words she was so scared that she "binged" her way to 120 pounds in one month. Everyone on her treatment team was happy except her. She was anxious, unhappy and depressed. She still felt "fat" and now had the proof that food made her "fat" and that the people around her wanted to her be "fat." She was afraid to eat to get "fat" and afraid to not eat because she was afraid of disappointing those around her. She was stuck, afraid and felt terribly alone. The beliefs she held around food all stemmed from being "good" or "bad" in her mind and her beliefs as to whether or not she was "good" or "bad" was linked to what she had eaten.

In beginning our work together, I first had to help her identify and define her feeling of "fat." As we say in my office, "fat is not a feeling but we can find what feeling fat defines for you." After working with this client to develop trust and rapport, which had been shattered from her previous experience, we began our work in identifying what her feeling of "fat" symbolized. In specific process with this client she identified that fat was her code word for fear. She was afraid of food, afraid of her eating disorder, afraid of those around her, afraid of herself, afraid of what she could be in her life and afraid of what she couldn't be. She was afraid of getting "fat" but couldn't define what fat was. She could define her fear in these other areas specifically and what it surrounded. Identifying these fear-based beliefs, and teaching her about beliefs in general, allowed her to understand they were beliefs based in an emotion and even though they appeared real, after some process in our work together she began to admit that some of them may not be.

As you can see, working with fear-based beliefs is different because these beliefs transfer into other beliefs. One belief bridges to another and without looking at the whole underlying belief construct, one cannot heal.

Fear-based beliefs are based in a perfectionist belief system that relates to various areas of a person's life. So, as well as bringing in new beliefs for a client, as a practitioner, you must also bring in self-compassion, gratitude and mindfulness. This allows the psyche to move out of fear. Fear cannot exist when someone has compassion for themselves, gratitude for their world and mindfulness in their life. I will regularly have clients work on these aspects of their self while we work on reconstructing their beliefs.

In working with Carole, the client mentioned above, we did intense work around mindfulness and gratitude in her life and with her food. Although clients with anorexia nervosa can find it difficult to find extreme gratitude and mindfulness with food, small, incremental steps help clients change radically. First we began with grounding tools to help her stay present in the moment for as long as she could. (Note that clients with severe malnutrition will have difficulty being able to ground for lengthy periods of time due to the brain's lack of protein and calorie intake. They can, however, begin to work on grounding to some degree so that when the malnutrition is healed they can continue to effectively practice this work with a nourished brain.) Then we worked with gratitude, having her focus on what she was grateful for in moments and then daily. This shifted her feelings from fear to gratitude and began to allow her brain to practice the shift from fear/anxiety to calm.

Mindfulness refers to the ability a person has to be present in the moment. In the last 21 years, both in the work on myself and the work that I do with clients, I have realized how mindless we are in our work and our lives. Being present, mindful, allows us to truly come into the moment. It is what allows us to be in the present instead of the future or the past. Without the skill to obtain and maintain presence, things like visualization, internal awareness and true choice in our lives are not possible.

In order to work on your mindfulness, focus on the different aspects of your emotional state table. Create a state of mindfulness, notice what you focus on, feel, your physiology and your self-talk. If you cannot focus on all of these to create this state, first focus on your breathing and other aspects of your physiology. This is the easiest way to begin learning how to ground, come into the present moment and be mindful. Breathe deep and slow and feel your feet on the ground. Start here and practice often five minutes a day three to four times a day. Just as a muscle needs to be exercised, our skill in grounding/mindfulness needs to be exercised as well. This builds the neural synapses in the brain and allows for the ability to ground become greater and easier to achieve as practice prevails.

It is very important to note that if a fear-based belief is worked on solely without looking at the whole perfectionist belief construct the person will move this construct somewhere else. The belief of "I am fat" that equates to "I am not good enough" can transfer into any aspect of a client's life. It prevents clients from ever feeling a sense of self-acceptance/love and continues to keep fear as a prevailing emotion surrounding their belief construct(s).

At its core, this is what leads to cross-addiction, someone who stops restricting and begins using alcohol or drugs or vice versa. In my practice, approximately 30 percent of my clients have presented with a cross-addiction. Most of my clients have come to treatment with me when their eating disorder behaviors increased after they received treatment for alcoholism. There are some others that have come to treatment after abstaining from drugs or sex. So they stopped using alcohol or other addictive habits but returned back to using their eating disorder. Proving the fact that the perfectionist belief construct needs to be annihilated to help with lasting, transformative healing.

Shame-Based Beliefs

Shame-based beliefs are different from fear-based beliefs. Shame is an overriding transformative emotion that prevails when an individual has either been raised in shame and/or continues to keep shame as a prevalent emotion around them in their lives presently. There is a tremendous difference between shame and guilt that is worth noting here.

Guilt is a feeling that we have for a few moments that allows us to consider negative consequences of an ACTION we have done. It exists in order to keep us and those around us safe.

Shame, on the other hand, is the feeling that prevails in an individual's psyche or soul regularly surrounding WHO they are, NOT what they do.

For example, if a person is speeding and gets pulled over by the police the individual who says, "Darn, I was going too fast, I wish I wouldn't have DONE that" displays the feeling of guilt. It will stop them from speeding next time and make them slow down to abide by the law. Guilt is an emotion that changes our action(s); it lasts a short period of time and only relates to the specific action that we did.

Conversely, a person who gets pulled over by the same policeman who says, "I am so stupid. I always do the wrong things. Why am I such a ..." uses language that focuses on the whole individual, not the action. This language is a prime example of shame. Shame is pervasive, long-lasting and transitions from one situation to the next.

The difference between shame and guilt is exemplified as well in parental language, by telling a child they are "a bad boy" or "a bad girl" versus "what you did was bad or wrong." In essence, the difference lies in the "I am," which equates to shame, versus the "I do," which equates to guilt.

Childhood experiences of shame shape who we are and how we relate to ourselves. Shame creates beliefs that change who we are and how we think about ourselves and our world. Shame-based beliefs destroy our sense of self-worth and worthiness. They are an intensely painful experience of believing we are flawed and therefore unworthy of love from ourselves and others.

Brené Brown, who is a shame researcher, has identified 12 categories of shame. They are:
- Appearance and Body Image
- Money and Work

- Motherhood/Fatherhood
- Family
- Parenting
- Mental and Physical Health
- Addiction
- Sex
- Aging
- Religion
- Surviving Trauma
- Being Stereotyped or Labeled

The distinct difference in shame-based beliefs lies in the fact that shame definitively creates identity-based beliefs. Beliefs such as "I am not worthy," "I am not good enough," "I am not enough." Whenever a belief starts with "I am" it is an identity-based belief and dictates how we feel about ourselves at the core.

Pervasive, entrenching and overwhelming, they control how we filter our experience in the world and dictate how we act with ourselves and with those around us. Shame-based beliefs, particularly when they are based in trauma, may present as one thing on the surface but may be a metaphor or analogy of something underlying related to the shame in the trauma. A specific example of a shame based belief is "I am dirty." This belief presents as one thing on the surface but ultimately leads to other beliefs layered in shame and relates to how an individual views themselves in general but relates truly to an underlying pervasive feeling.

Ally, a 37-year-old self-employed successful business owner, came to me for coaching to bring her business to the next level to increase her financial income. In talking with her in our first session, she began to cry in speaking about her previous fiancé. She began to recount how she had cheated on him and in that contracted a sexually transmitted disease that she then infected him with. Not only did she impact her health but the health of her fiancé and the long-term implications for future relations for both as her fiancé immediately decided to break up with her. "I am so dirty" was a belief that came up over and over again in our initial session.

In our second session we dove into that belief and her feelings behind it. After some education and understanding, she identified the feeling of shame that was behind this belief and how this belief related to her feeling of being "dirty" in some things that happened that were sexually inappropriate when she was younger. So the belief of being dirty really had nothing to do with being unclean but had to do with the feeling of shame she felt around the consequences of her sexual promiscuity, both in the past and presently.

In the third session we dove more into the present belief and the most recent issue that happened to keep her in the moment as much as possible. We looked at the belief of being dirty and tried to identify it. I asked her what was actually the feeling of dirty? What is another way you could look at this situation? What belief would allow you to feel clean, whole?

In processing this she came out and said, "My gynecologist says that what I have is just dermatitis."

"Really," I said. "What if it were just dermatitis?"

We spoke about that at length for the next few minutes to see how that felt for her. Before we finished our session I asked her, "Would you consider re-creating this belief?" and "What would prevent you from creating a new belief?" She told me she would seriously consider this and we hung up.

At 3 p.m. the next day I received a text from Ally. It stated, "After we got off the phone I really thought about what you said and went to bed considering different beliefs. Honestly, Wendi, you were right, it IS just dermatitis, a skin disorder. It's nothing more than that. In believing this I feel free to date and create a new life again. This belief allows me to be and feel free."

Since she has taken on this new belief, we have been able to dive into grounding and working in the present with this new belief. As she has owned this new belief she has also completed goals for her business financially and geographically, confronted business financial issues and completed business financial goals. She has also completed massive organization within her home and within her small business. In her freedom, she is truly alive and ready to tackle what she needs to in her business and her life.

This client truly exemplifies courage in facing her shame-based belief and has experienced much positive fulfillment in crafting her new belief. Whether your disempowering belief is based in fear, shame or another emotion, re-creating a new one will absolutely change your life. A new belief allows your story to be empowered in the future and your emotional state to be proactive instead of reactive.

CHAPTER 7

THE MEANINGS OF OUR LIVES

> "Meanings are not determined by situations,
> but we determine ourselves by the meanings
> we give to situations."
> — Alfred Alder

As beliefs are the "cake" to our lives, meanings are the icing on top of the cake. Meanings are the support in words that surround our belief systems. Like beliefs, meanings are created unconsciously and automatically. Identifying and then shifting beliefs will also infinitely affect the meanings you create from the stories in your life.

There are two types of meanings that we create from the events that occur in our life. The first type is the meaning we give to a pattern of events. For example, if parents are continually busy with work a child may perceive this to mean that they are not important. These meanings directly become some type of belief construct, depending on the situation.

The second type of meaning is the meaning we give to external (events in the world) or internal (such as thoughts, feelings and memories) events. These meanings last only as long as the event lasts. After the event discontinues the memory meaning we store based on the event is the one that exists. It is this memory meaning (or the meaning we give to the memory we remember) that creates the belief construct derived from this event. Since most of us never distinguish between actual and perceived events we realistically place the meaning and ultimately the belief that is derived from this event based on our perceived memory and meaning.

For example, if a friend walks into a room and doesn't speak to us, and this event means to us "my friend doesn't like me," it seems to us as if the reality is my friend doesn't like me. At which point we deal with this person as if he really doesn't like me, when the reality is that when he walked into the room he did not talk to us. In other words, because we usually don't distinguish between an event and the meaning we give the event, we deal with the meaning as if it is what actually happened.

Myla, who came to me with restrictive anorexia, purging and compulsive exercise at the age of 16 on referral from her therapist, began working with me to help her heal from her eating disorder, anxiety, compulsive exercise and radical self-loathing. Although she was an extremely beautiful girl, externally she never saw this and only focused on and saw her flaws. During our first session we identified together that she would only allow herself to eat 5 grams or less of fat per day, eat less than 1200 calories per day and needed to exercise at least 90 minutes per day. When she wasn't working out she was studying to achieve the highest grades possible to allow her to get into the college she wanted to go to. As she was in a very competitive high school, this constituted approximately 4-6 hours of studying per night.

She believed that if she ate anything different she would become fat. If she did anything different with studying she would fail. She exercised to help with her anxiety, fear and anger. In speaking about her mother's beliefs she identified that her mother would not eat anything with fat in it and would only consume a "certain" number of calories according to her mother's continual "diet." Both her mom and dad were perpetually "dieting" and exercising to "control" their weight. Being thin was a primary vehicle of approval in this house, and anything less than that was not acceptable. (Until Myla was diagnosed with anorexia I don't think they ever saw their own behavior or those of her daughter as detrimental. Even months after our work began I had to work with her parents around their beliefs and the translation to Myla.) This created multiple beliefs for Myla with a primary meaning of life to be that if you don't keep things "under control" you weren't successful. Success to Myla, based on her parents beliefs and actions, meant perfection. Perfection ultimately would mean that you would receive love and approval from those around you.

I remember one distinct session with this client where I had commented on her great sense of humor. For a few moments she looked at me without speaking and finally said, "No one has ever commented on anything I have personality-wise. Everyone only always comments on my body or how pretty I am. You are the first person in 16 years that has ever said anything about who I am." Truth or not, her perception was her reality and in that I felt quite sad for her that she had never truly felt love or accepted for who she was. This conversation ultimately led to a whole other set of beliefs and meanings we uncovered and transformed related to the person whom she thought she was versus the person she actually was. It wasn't just the beliefs she had but the meanings she created from these beliefs that were holding her hostage.

CHAPTER 8

PUTTING IT ALL TOGETHER: THE EBM SYSTEM (EMOTION, BELIEFS AND MEANINGS)

"An old belief is like an old shoe. We so value its comfort that we fail to notice the hole in it."
-Robert Brault

Stories, beliefs, emotions and meanings are all components of our identity.

Story--Beliefs--Emotions--Meanings

IDENTITY

Crafting and changing our beliefs ultimately changes not just our emotions and meanings related to our stories but ultimately affects our identity in our world. Identity is the "I am" of who we are. Identity is a combination of all of the stories, beliefs, emotions and meanings and it creates how we act and interact in the world. It is our definition of who we are.

An example of this for a client with Restrictive Anorexia Nervosa:

Story: My mom criticizes herself when she eats high-calorie food.

Belief: If I eat high-calorie foods my mom will not love me.

Emotion: Fear.

Meaning: Being overweight and eating foods that can make you gain weight means no one will love you.

Identity: I am a person who doesn't eat high-calorie foods.

An example for a person with Compulsive Overeating:

Story: Every time I go on a diet I can't complete it.

Belief: I am weak.

Emotion: Anger.

Meaning: I will never be able to lose weight. I am destined to be fat.

Identity: I am a failure.

There are more organizing constructs behind this linking system for most of my clients with some facet of an eating disorder. For example, eliminated or bad foods for each client vary greatly or the amount of weight they can or will be at varies greatly as well.

This linking system is not only for those with a diagnosis; it happens for all of us in our daily lives.

For a small business owner unable to expand their business:

Story: Every time I try to expand my business it doesn't work.

Belief: I am a failure.

Emotions: Sadness/frustration.

Meaning: No matter how much marketing I do I can't grow my business. Maybe I am not meant to be a _____.

Identity: I am a terrible business person.

By working with this business owner's belief of "I am a terrible coach, chiropractor, therapist, dentist," I can help him/her to shift the belief, which changes the emotion and creates a new meaning and therefore identity. It works in synchronistic fashion as changing the belief enables the others to open and change.

If we look at this linking system as the "sunflower of identity," you can see how beliefs are at the core of this system and the part that affects the other systems the most.

In changing the middle of the flower we change the other parts of the sunflower. As the middle changes or dies it kills the outer petals both green and yellow.

> *When Kaiya was first diagnosed and I was spiraling I didn't realize that I began to construct a meaning that revolved around paying back "karma" for things I had done. I began to feel like things were happening to me/us. I started to re-create stories of what I had done or hadn't done in the past and found meaning based on these beliefs, although disempowering, in this universal principal. I linked it to what I had/hadn't done with and for my mother as well as continually assessing what I had or had not done for other people in my life as well. I searched for any meaning I could find.*
>
> *I also began to wonder "when will something else happen," continually searching for when the other shoe*

would drop. I moved into hypervigilance and constriction. I began to focus on what things were going wrong and forgot to focus on what was going right. I constructed meaning about the independent events that were occurring in my life and linking them in a pattern to find some type of meaning. In effect, however, I was pulling from a disempowering construct of universality.

When I reworked my beliefs this meaning of the events dissolved. I was able to take each event in its own lesson and accord and not create a meaning linking this pattern. Furthermore, as I became stronger and pushed myself further in life, in my professional training and in my personal growth, I found an even more empowering belief that I still keep with me today. In my life, I now truly believe and know that the universe is working for me. In this, I know that everything is right as it should be when, where and how it happens.

I have also reworked my beliefs and meanings regarding my mother's illness. Earlier in the book I alluded to my mother's battle with alcoholism, mental illness and prescription drug addiction. She raised me as a single mom and although she used alcohol regularly as I was growing up, she was able to hold a job to allow us to have an apartment, food and clothing with some extras in there as well.

In looking back at my life when I was younger I can absolutely see the signs of mental illness in my mother as well her noted alcoholism. In the last 10-15 years as my mom's mental illness and addiction has gotten greater she has been unable to be in my children's lives regularly. For the first few years of my children's lives this created great sadness for me. I often felt as if I was a motherless daughter, even though my mother was still alive. Our lack of relationship to me meant that I was to have to handle life on my own, that my life was not designed to have a mother figure or "family." At times I felt grief and sadness based on these beliefs and meanings, which escalated during this time with Kaiya.

A few years ago, as I was reworking how I looked at my life, I realized that my definition of family and a "mom" was based on a traditional definition. In looking at my life, it has been anything but traditional. I then wondered how I could define an empowering belief and meaning about having a mom and family focused on my own definition. I began to focus on other "mother" figures I had in my life and other "family" members. I focused on what I had instead of what I did not have. In that I realized that in continuing to believe that I had no mom and no family I was disempowering myself.

It was then I made the choice, through lots of readings and self-actualizations, to become empowered. I focused on my family in front of me—my own children and husband. I focused on the family and mother figures I had in my life that had helped raise me or had been on the perimeter of my world—my grandfather, my cousins, my great-aunt, my stepmom, stepsister and stepbrother, and my amazing friends. In looking at all this I began to truly believe that I had been given all that I needed through my life in having what I needed from those around me. I began to believe that in what I had I was truly abundant in love from those that did surround me. I began to believe and know now that the "universe was and always has been working for me and in that it has provided everything I needed in that moment and more."

CHAPTER 9

TURNING DISEMPOWERMENT AROUND: THE "HOW TO" GUIDE TO EMPOWERMENT

> "Turn your wounds into wisdom."
> – Oprah Winfrey

The definition of empowerment, for review, is being able to be in true choice in your life which allows you to define your outcome or results. In this, we know that the first step is being **in choice**. The first steps I will focus on in this section will enable you and your clients to be in true choice from a grounded perspective. The second part will focus on a process of outcome or result writing (a process I call OR) and the third section will put everything together in the EBM technique. This technique takes an individual's beliefs and deconstructs and reconstructs them in order to truly empower a client to create lasting change.

A Side Note: Trust and Rapport

Note that in working with your own clients, prior to any of these processes being completed you must establish trust and rapport. Without this, none of these or any other processes will be transformative for a client or yourself.

In order to establish trust and build rapport you must see your client's model of the world. What is important to them? What do they love? What do they hate? What do they focus on? How do they best relate to others and how do they not relate to others? What do they want to focus on in their work with you? Why did they come to see you? Questions allow you to really open up and understand where a client lives, not geographically, but emotionally, authentically. They allow you to identify, construct and understand a model of the client's world.

Rapport is a state of harmonious understanding with another individual or group that enables greater and easier communication. Matching and mirroring a client in their body language, eye contact, facial expressions and voice tone/tempo allows clients to identify with you and creates deep rapport. If you work with clients on the phone this constitutes mainly matching and mirroring their voice tone and tempo as well as their energy level and pace of wording. In working with my clients in person I match and mirror their body language or use body language that relates to them. Interestingly for me this was never originally intentional on my part, it was just something I did. So, if a client sat a certain way I might follow and sit the same way or vice versa. If they began using their hands while talking I might do that as well. What I never realized was this skillset, called empathic, worked to my advantage to establish trust and rapport with my clients very quickly. For me, it comes naturally, a facet of my personality, but if it does not for you, make it intentional and learn more about it. It absolutely enables the client to feel connected on a deeper level to you.

Baby, Big Steps: Grounding, Breathing and Breath Work

Breathing is always the first step in going through any type of change process. Although we all feel like we breathe every day, it is very common in my work with my clients that I find their breathing is not really true, full breathing. Their nervous system is commonly in hypervigilance and their body in constrictive physiological patterns.

Deep, full breathing relieves stress and anxiety due to its physiological effect on the nervous system. Breathing slowly and mindfully activates the hypothalamus, connected to the pituitary gland in the brain, to send out neurohormones that inhibit stress-producing hormones and trigger a relaxation response in the body. The hypothalamus links the nervous system to the endocrine system, which secretes the hormones that regulate all activities throughout the body. What this means in non-biochemical terms is that breath provides relaxation and the body to reduce stress radically.

If a person takes shallow breaths which creates a stress-related response, the adrenal medulla (or what people call the adrenals) secretes epinephrine and norepinephrine which further increases breathing rate, heart rate and blood pressure which moves the body into fight-or-flight response. This, in turn creates more stress within the body, moving the brain and body in a continual breathing and physiology pattern. The one way to counteract this process from occurring is by using grounding techniques that utilize breath work.

Dr. Andrew Weil states that the breath functions as a link between the unconscious and conscious mind, a tool to influence the involuntary nervous system, a technique to decrease anxiety and increase spiritual awareness and development, ground the mind, body and spirit and increase communication pathways between the mind/body connection. I would add that it can also be used to relieve pain and increase creativity and intuition.

The Simplest Strategy for Grounding and Breath Work

Grounding is a coping strategy that is designed to "ground" you in or immediately connect you with the present moment. One of the easiest ways I teach my clients to ground and use breath work is in the simplest, most effective format.

1. First, stop and sit down with your feet planted directly on the floor. Your feet must be firmly planted on the floor and not dangling or touching only in one section. I have found for some clients as well that some of them may feel most grounded standing in a strong, standing pose with their feet firmly planted.
2. Notice whether you feel most comfortable closing your eyes or keeping them open focusing on a center point.
3. Third, take one long deep breath in. As your chest rises try to feel your lungs inflate with air. Take in as much air as possible.
4. As you release this air out of your lungs notice and begin to feel your feet on the ground. Notice which parts you can feel. Can you feel your toes? The balls of your feet? Or the heels of your feet?
5. Repeat 2-3 more times until you can feel all components on your feet and that they are firmly planted on the ground.

Complex Facets of Grounding

Other grounding techniques often use the five senses (sound, touch, smell, taste and sight) and breath to immediately connect people with the here and now; for example, listening to loud music and singing while using breath in this process. Touching a stone (called a touchstone) while using a process similar to what I have written above or holding onto a piece of ice while breathing are also ways that a person can ground themselves. The latter techniques all produce sensations that are difficult to ignore, thereby directly and instantaneously connecting you with the present moment.

Another great example of a grounding technique is called the 54321 game.

Take a deep breath in and let it out.
1. Name 5 things you can see in the room with you.
2. Take a deep breath in and let it out.
3. Name 4 things you can feel ("chair on my back" or "feet on floor").
4. Take a deep breath in and let it out.
5. Name 3 things you can hear right now ("fingers tapping on keyboard" or "TV").
6. Take a deep breath in and let it out
7. Name 2 things you can smell right now (or 2 things you like the smell of).
8. Take a deep breath in and let it out.
9. Name 1 good thing about yourself—be specific.

Breathing and grounding are the first steps to allow a client or yourself to make lasting change. It allows us to stand in choice around our emotional state and strategies or choices that we are presented with. Without grounding and breath work nothing can change because we are not in true choice, unable to be present in the moment. This step, in any format, should be completed prior to doing any type of change process outlined in this book.

Next Step: Orienting

Orienting is a process of becoming aware of our location in time and space. Orienting can be used to help a client ground and be in their place/space before, during or after a traumatic event, in a new environment with excessive stimulation, or in an environment with excessive amounts of change.

When I sat with my father as he was passing away in the hospital many years ago, I used orienting continuously as a coping strategy. I know that orienting during this process created radical empowerment for me as I had the most amazing experience in his passing and was able to help talk him through his process of crossing over. In this I was also able to maintain my state of gratitude and love and amazing memories from these moments of love and joy instead of grief or anger.

Orienting Process
1. In the moment, move to a place where you are centered physiologically, either sitting or standing in strong pose. Be aware that no one in your environment has to know what you are doing.
2. Take a deep, full breath in and allow your mind to focus on your feet. Feel the base of your feet—the balls of your feet, mid-feet, and soles of feet.
3. Next, take another full deep breath and feel your calves and upper legs.

4. Continue to breathe deep and full, and focus on your core/midsection and move up to shoulders, upper body and arms, so you have connected to each part of your body while you are breathing deep and full.
5. As you move to your head and neck, turn your neck all the way to look over your right shoulder and spot one thing in your environment. Breathe deeply and notice what you see.
6. Then, move your head and neck slightly to the left so that you are looking at a 45-degree angle, between your shoulder and center field of vision. Breathe deeply and notice what you see.
7. Next, move your head and neck to center and notice what you see and breathe deeply.
8. Continue to move your head and neck all the way to the left. Breathe deeply and notice what you see.
9. Finally, move your head and neck to a 45-degree angle on the left side. Breathe deeply and notice what you see.
10. Go back to center and take a deep, full breath, being fully aware of what was spotted at each angle, being now fully aware of your environment and being able to know, focus and be present in the moment in the environment we are in.

The OR Process: Outcome/Result Writing

Defining your outcome/result in definite terms is one of the definitive facets to becoming empowered. Once you know all of your choices, defining your outcome or result for these choices is your next step. This allows you or your client to clearly identify the direction they are moving in. It will also allow you to have a barometer for where they are moving and if they are moving in the right direction. Measurement of results is the key to success.

OR Steps

1. What do you want? Or what does your client want?
    a. Be specific; exactly who, what, when, where, why and how.
    b. State in positive terms: don't state what you don't want, state what you DO want.
    c. Must be self-directed. The outcome can only be about you and for you. It can only be about what the client can truly control or have containment over. Therefore, it cannot include making someone act a certain way, unless that someone is themselves.
    d. Double-check if it is achievable or realistic. Losing 25 pounds in 7 days is not a realistic goal. Make sure you or your client is not setting themselves up for failure.
    e. Must be for your greater good. Double-check that the outcome is enhancing empowerment, adding to choices and quality of life. Find someone to double-check this and/or double-check this with yourself. This is where an awesome coach, therapist or dietitian can look from a heartfelt space at the client's long-term vision and see if this specifically fits.
    f. If the outcome is result oriented, state all the results. For example, if the outcome is weight loss, don't just state the amount of pounds to be released, put all other results that will accompany this. Potentially feeling strong in your body, having a better connection with your body,

enjoying the freedom of movement, playing with your children or grandchildren, enjoying hikes in nature, etc.

2. Why do you want this? Truly, at your core, why do you want this outcome? Allow the emotional connection of this outcome to come to fruition, letting your heart direct this part of the process instead of your head. (Actually, it would be your amygdala instead of your frontal brain; see section on brain and emotions.) Remember, emotion leads us into motion. As human beings we connect to emotion. Emotion leads to motion. It's why we buy products, do things for others in need and stay up too late at night watching the end of a close football game. Without emotion, achieving your result or outcome will only be sustainable for so long. To create change that lasts we must connect to the emotion involved. A perfect example is releasing 50 pounds into the universe will allow me to have freedom in all aspects of my life, freedom to play with my children, freedom to go where I want to go when I want to go, freedom to buy clothes where I want to, joy in being able to roll down the hill with my children, strength in being able to know that I achieved accomplishment in this area of my life. For practitioners, this would also be the time to check out if there is any negative emotion or emotion that is holding back your client at this time. Notice and uncover if there is any facet of fear, anger, frustration or loss that surfaces. If so, now is the time to work with that before you go further.

3. Put #1 and #2 together in writing and check it out. Stand up, shake your body out and reread it. See how it feels. Where do you feel it in your body? For practitioners this is the part of the exercise where you would ultimately be able to help your clients determine if this outcome/result is viewed as a threat or is centered in their core. Is it positive in their mind but a threat in their body? There have been a number of times when I have written outcomes with clients who have thought their outcome was congruent with their whole being, and when we checked it out they actually felt that their throat was tightening and they were choking. In this case we reworked their OR, as it was connecting to a part of them that was not positive and would be difficult to sustain.

4. The next step is measurement. How will you know when you have achieved your goal? What will achieving this goal look like in your world? Look at all the results that could be measured. For example, would you be able to laugh more, feel more alive, wear a different size clothing, have energy to hike twice a week and communicate with your spouse effectively around your needs?

5. How will achieving this affect yourself and others? Look at all of the positive ways achieving this will work within your life personally and professionally. How will it affect those around you in your life, your spouse, children, co-workers, business, etc.?

6. Sit down, breathe and visualize this. Play it out like a movie on a movie screen in your head. How will other

people relate to you? How will their faces look? What will you be able to do differently? How will it really look "real time"? Is there anything you want to add, change or delete? Notice how this movie makes you feel. Where do you feel it? How do you feel it? For professionals this is another place where you can help your client by slowing them down in this part of the process in grounding and noticing what this movie is like for them to be aware of truly how it impacts them in their world. Once the movie is complete and you are feeling empowered—and not before—move to step 7.

7. Write down what has prevented you from doing this in the past. What obstacles have stood in your way? Is it your story? Is it your emotional state? Has it been your strategy for attacking this outcome or result? What are your potential saboteurs? For a great resource on identifying your saboteurs read the book *Positive Intelligence* by Shirzad Chamine. What have your obstacles been in the past? What are the solutions? State them clearly and effectively in positive, solution-focused language.

8. What personal or professional resources do you need? Not just material resources but emotional, physiological and intellectual resources. What resources do you already have? What resources do you need to seek out and find? For example, if you are trying to build your business but do not have a good financial infrastructure for your business or an accountant, one of the first resources you will need to seek is a good small business accountant. For a client with an eating disorder it might be a treatment team.

9. Finally, write final outcome with emotion and a visual. A visual representation of what this final outcome will feel like is imperative to enact the unconscious mind. It is also important to enact the auditory component of the brain as well, selecting a song or sound that represents the feeling that this outcome/result will hold for you specifically. Remember your movie—what parts or pieces of it can you recreate on your paper? Is there a picture or visual symbol that reminds you of this outcome/result? Is there a song that was playing in your movie? Include on this final draft solutions or visuals of solutions as well.

10. Put it all together in your environment. Can you have it as a screen saver on your computer, on your phone, on a poster board? You can have your visuals in images or symbols around your house as reminders as well. I had a client once who was working on her triad of choice/freedom and had triangles in various forms all around her house. Play your song or auditory sound, frequently connecting to the emotion surrounding this outcome/result. Doing these three things engages all three facets of the brain—front, middle and back brain—radically increasing opportunity for success.

Once in true choice, grounded, oriented and you have now written your outcome or result, you and/or your clients can then continue the process of working with beliefs and belief constructs to continue the empowerment process.

A Case Study—Samantha's Story

Samantha was a client that came to me for coaching around life issues that were taking place in her life with her older child who had just began an outpatient treatment program for drug addiction. During the time of Sam raising her children and throughout her son's issue with drugs she had lost sight of her priorities, the number one of these being her weight as it had steadily increased over the course of the last 20 years due to her emotional overeating patterns.

After working with some life and emotional state issues to stabilize Sam, we began writing her OR for changing her relationship with food and losing weight. She first defined her outcome as weight loss. We then started working through the OR process and ignited her true OR as being in a size 12 clothing within the next three months by decreasing her overeating by 80% and increasing her fiber intake. This would allow her to fit into her clothes better, feeling good as she went to work, enjoy her body more, increase her energy to be able to play with her grandchild and feel stronger emotionally. She was able to fully connect to the emotion of strength as she had felt perpetually "weak" in this area of her life for many years and truly desired to discover the contrary feeling. This OR focused not just on the amount of weight she would lose but on her entire emotional, physical and psychological patterns, enabling her to connect into every facet of empowerment and success.

Discovering and Uncovering Beliefs

Just as developing a belief has a process, discovering and uncovering beliefs has a process as well. Discovering beliefs is the first process prior to transformation and can be done either with yourself or with a practitioner.

Discovering and Uncovering Belief Process for Yourself
1. Complete a 24-hour log of all things you say to yourself during the day. This can either be out loud or internally. During this time you can also ask trusted friends or family members if they hear you say things regularly as well.
2. As you go through the second day, notice and note how many of those things you say throughout this day. Use hashmarks for repeat beliefs that show up so you can delineate which beliefs primarily show up for you.
3. On the third day, sit and circle all of those dialogues that you realize are beliefs. Sometimes our internal language are not beliefs but other facets of self-talk related to focused belief. For example, saying I don't know how anybody likes me may not necessarily be a belief but would be related to another belief construct such as I am unlikeable.
4. Which of these beliefs do you want to keep and which do you want to shed? Which ones serve or help you in your life and which of those do not?
5. Prioritize these based on the one(s) you want to change first or which one(s) you feel are most damaging.
6. Move on to the EBM process with the first belief.

Discovering and Uncovering Belief Process as a Practitioner
1. Notice and be aware of client's language and write beliefs as you hear them and circle them in your notes.
2. Allow client to complete 24-hour log as mentioned above and bring to session. Have them put log aside and bring to next session to discuss. If appropriate have them email you log so that you may review prior to session.

3. Ask your client what beliefs do you want to keep? What beliefs do you want to change?
4. Prioritize with client. Really dive into each belief and find which one of these is truly detrimental. Which beliefs are related to the issues you are working with them on? Which beliefs are truly detrimental to their psyche? Which beliefs will affect them long-term and short-term? Create the client's priority list.
5. Next, teach your client about beliefs in specific so they can understand what they are, where they come from and how they will benefit from changing these.
6. State belief number one. Clarify and verify belief to enable client and yourself to truly know exactly what belief you are working on and what benefit working on this belief will have. Really look at the clients compelling reason why for changing this belief and their ultimate result. This will create their compelling why—their emotional reason to change.
7. Finally, ask them some questions around this belief to probe further. Are they open to changing this belief? Is there any resistance to changing this belief? How does this work for them in their life? How does this belief impact them or those around them negatively in their life?
8. Move onto the EBM process with this first belief.

A Side Note: Working with Stories

The first process in discovering and uncovering beliefs is to investigate where and how these beliefs were created. Beliefs can be created during an event or from the created memory of an event. Our "story" is a chain of events linked together around a series of events that is either reality or our created reality.

In working with a story that has created beliefs an individual wants to change you can first look at the story behind the beliefs. In doing so you can decide to change or craft the story or memory of the chain of events.

1. Create a movie in your mind that shows the story as you remember. See it as if you were sitting in a movie theater. Allow the movie to play in black and white. Then let it replay in color. Rewind and fast forward the movie as you want to enable you to feel mastery over this story. Stop the movie at the moment of the event that created the belief and ask yourself: What would you change about this movie? How would you change it? How would that have changed the belief?
2. What resources would you need to have in this story to have it change? **A resource is something needed to create a different outcome.** Be as creative or imaginative as possible. If you needed to have a superhero come in and change the movie do that. Focus on the aspects of the movie that are changeable. What is the feeling or emotional state that you would have wanted in this movie? How or what would you need to change in order to change the belief that was created?
3. Change the movie and play it with the resource you needed to change the belief.
4. Notice how it feels in your mind and in your emotional state. Does it change your emotional state about the story? What do you notice about the change in your emotional state?
5. Next, notice how it feels in your body, your physiology. Where do you feel this movie in your body? Where do you feel this emotional state in your body?

6. Now, conclude if this movie creates the outcome you needed to change the belief and emotional state related to this story.
7. If it does, run the crafted movie from beginning to end in color, linking the new empowering belief and meaning to the story.

Note: As a practitioner you can do this visualization with your clients, slow it down and tailor it specifically to clients' needs, continually making sure that clients are grounded and oriented during the process.

The EBM Process

Once beliefs are identified and prioritized, transformation occurs in using the EBM process. True belief transformation ignites your true self, radically transforming your life and the lives of those you love around you.

1. Use grounding and orienting techniques noted prior to allow clients to be oriented in their setting and grounding in their physiology.
2. Go back and state the identified belief you or your client want to transform. Does this belief serve your life purpose and those around you?
3. Now, construct a question around this belief. For example, in the belief "I am not worthy," the question becomes "Is it really true that I am not worthy?" or "What am I actually not worthy of?" Or the example of "I am not a good business man/woman," the question becomes "Is it really true that I am not a good business man/woman?"
4. Identify the positive intention behind this belief. Even if the belief is not positive, the intention behind creating

it was positive at the time it was created. Why did you/your client create this belief? For example, the belief of being unworthy may have the intention of keeping someone in an emotional state that is congruent with their surroundings. When a client's parents are unable to own or accept greatness from those around them, being in a state of unworthiness allows the client to be congruent with their parents' beliefs, allowing them to be acceptable in their environment.

5. Do you need to continue with this intention? Are there other ways that you can complete this intention? If there were other ways would you be willing to look at them?
6. Poke holes in the current belief. Is this true 100% of the time? Really, why is this true? How is it true? The question "Why?" is one of the most useful ways to begin to truly put doubt around a belief.
7. Reframe the belief. Write the belief in two parts to break it down. I am-----unworthy. Reframe unworthy to what the client specifically wants/needs to believe about him or herself. Now ask, what would you need to believe in order to achieve the outcome you want/need? I would need to belief that I deserved greatness. Remember to notice what type of belief it is based on in the beginning part of belief. In this example it is an identity-based belief. Education on the types of beliefs can be important for clients understanding and knowledge of beliefs and their patterns.
8. Develop and write this belief specifically.
9. Check and test for ecology. Have the client stand up or sit down in a comfortable position after they have taken a moment to reground themselves. Read the new belief

out loud. Now ask the client one or all of these three questions. Where they feel the new belief in their body? What emotional state does this new belief allow you to have? With this new belief are you capable of doing everything you desire (your purpose)? If the new belief allows the client to link to emotional state, outcome or result they desire and enables them to link to an empowered feeling in their body, the belief has been transformed. If the belief leads to a disempowering feeling, restart with step number 2 and dive further into this belief to see if there is a belief hiding underneath; this is so with fear- or shame-based beliefs.

10. Have client re-read the belief at least three times out loud so that they can work out the language, grammar and content so that it feels exactly right.
11. Finally, take the belief in written format and put it in your environment on a notecard, sticky note or other written format. Now sit with this new belief and identify what visual comes to your mind as you think of it. Maybe the vision of a mountain or the sea or someone standing in the middle of a field. Whatever the visual is find a picture of it and gather as many as possible to put where you will see them with the written belief as well. You can also link this new belief to a song or music that supports this belief. Practice your new belief at least 5-10 times per day, saying it to yourself, playing the song and looking at your visual. Doing all three of these engages both the conscious and unconscious mind and will allow you to have all parts of your brain engaged in the process.
12. In order to fully engage your physiology, remember to feel the music, belief and visual identified in a certain area of your body. This anchors both the belief and

emotion somatically, allowing you to have unconscious access to this belief on all levels.

Steps number 3, 4, 5 and 6 allow the psyche to open up to specific change and to stay out of judgment of belief construct. It allows for change to be easy without negative charge or energy.

CHAPTER 10

YOUR NEXT STEPS AND RESOURCES

In reconstructing these beliefs, my meanings, emotions, stories and identity have shifted. I know that I am protected, loved and abundant in that I feel truly grateful for all that I have and all that I will receive. My knowing in all of this allows me to encompass my original belief that I held when I was younger that everything I have learned and do learn in my life creates learning for others. I am a conduit for learning and now I am immensely grateful for this and all that I have.

I know that if I could do this, you can do this and more as well. Life is about change and living and growing. Not just for yourself but for those around you. In taking your learning from this book you can continue to create massive and lasting change by reaching out to me for individual or group coaching for yourself as a client or for yourself as a professional, in a process called mentoring/supervision. You can also hire me to come and speak at your organization or small group. I love what I do and would love to continue to inspire and ignite massive lasting change with and for you and for those around you.

My intention in writing this book was to create a format for people to begin to understand what beliefs and true empowerment are and to start the healing process. I or someone on my team can help set up an appointment for you either in person or virtually.

For further information on individual or group sessions, mentoring/supervision, business coaching, nutrition therapy and speaking engagements, please contact me at 843-408-0340 or visit:

www.empowermentcoachinginternational.com

You can also access the last 20 pages of this book in workbook format on my website for further learning and self-exploration as well.

Here's to you and your courage in shattering those beliefs which prevent you from discovering, transforming and igniting your true self!

ABOUT THE AUTHOR

WENDI FRANCIS MS, RD/LDN, CPC
INTERVENTION NEUROSTRATEGIST

Wendi Francis is a certified life coach, speaker, neurostrategist, author, and recognized nutrition therapist. She has worked for over twenty years with clients by empowering them to overcome their fears and beliefs, as well as by developing new paradigms and a love for life. She guides her clients in breaking through their obstacles by looking at their values, beliefs, life purpose, emotions, previous traumas, and somatic experiences.

By incorporating her client's visuals, linguistics, and psychodynamic experiences they transform their system of function into an empowering position. Wendi's varied background and training allows her to use multiple skill sets and techniques to enable her clients to achieve their goals.

With decades of experience, Wendi has spoken on various topics, primarily women's empowerment, adolescent nutrition, trauma and food-related issues, food texture issues, eating disorders and weight management.

Wendi's personal experience as a home-school mom and a mother of a child with a chronic disease allows her to incorporate not only her professional knowledge into her practice and talks but also enables her to truly empathize and understand a caregiver's roles and responsibilities. She is a wife, mother of three, a yogi, runner, avid hiker and overall nature lover. Her practice and passion is helping empower others in her purpose-driven, results-focused and wellness oriented philosophy.

Made in the USA
Middletown, DE
08 June 2015